ONE WEEK LOAN

For Roger, Niels and Cassell,

with love

Planning Applications and Appeals

Helen Bryan

BUTTERWORTH
HEINEMANN

Butterworth-Heinemann
Linacre House, Jordan Hill, Oxford OX2 8DP
A division of Reed Educational and Professional Publishing Ltd

Ɽ A member of the Reed Elsevier plc group

OXFORD   BOSTON   JOHANNESBURG
MELBOURNE   NEW DELHI   SINGAPORE

First published 1996

© Helen Bryan 1996

Cartoons © Litza Jansz

Crown copyright is reproduced with the permission   L6
of the Controller of HMSO

British Library Cataloguing in Publication Data
A catalogue record for this book is available from the British Library

ISBN 0 7506 2792 1

Library of Congress Cataloguing in Publication Data
A catalogue record for this book is available from the Library of Congress

Printed and bound in Great Britain by
Biddles Ltd, Guildford and King's Lynn

Contents

Preface

The planning system regulates the development of our environment. While many people are concerned at the impact development has on their lives, most still demand 'development' in some form, or at least to enjoy its benefits. Thus people complain about traffic and pollution in urban and town centres, that new housing development on the outskirts of towns will lead to undesirable urban sprawls, that hostels for the homeless or sheltered accommodation for the mentally handicapped is not suitable in their neighbourhoods, that proposals for new shopping complexes or airports or nuclear power stations will destroy the countryside and create noise and pollution or are potentially dangerous.

Yet people also wish to have good access to transport between their homes, jobs and schools, and convenient shopping facilities. At the same time they want traffic routed out of town centres and away from residential areas. They wish proper sheltered accommodation to be provided if a family member should require it. In theory, many people favour some provision of emergency shelter for the homeless living on the streets, recreational facilities, youth clubs, or to see historic buildings put to some good use. They want cheap utilities and a transport system which will enable British goods and British labour to compete in European markets.

The vast majority of development proposals, from modest house extensions to major developments such as airports and motorways, will have some impact on the surrounding environment and a corresponding impact on people's lives.

What the planning system does is provide a mechanism for balancing society's requirements for development with wider social, economic and environmental considerations.

The system recognizes the necessity of development but ensures that the public can participate in its regulation. Effective use of the system depends on an understanding of the way that it operates. This is not the exclusive province of planning professionals such as solicitors, planning consultants, barristers, architects or surveyors although many people rely on their expertise.

Increasing numbers of people are seeking to use the planning system – they want to know whether they need apply for permission to extend a loft or turn a house into flats, what can be done about a proposal to demolish or alter an historic building, how to take part in a planning inquiry, how can possibly controversial development such as a shopping centre be facilitated or prevented, or how they can have a say in proposals for new motorways, airports or rail links, and in what circumstances might they be entitled to compensation if planning decisions have an adverse affect on their properties.

The system is designed to ensure that developers' proposals are considered fairly and that development is facilitated and encouraged subject to such appropriate considerations or restrictions as may apply. At the same time, the system recognizes the wider public interest in development and provides a means for interested parties to be heard in the process of development regulation.

This book is designed to explain both how the system works and how to use it. It is a practical guide to the basic procedures of the planning system and the general principles which govern the development process. As such the book should prove a useful guide, of use to non-professionals, professionals and students alike.

Note to readers

Because this book is written with the lay reader in mind, I have intentionally avoided references to specific sections of the statutes or policy documents referred to, for three reasons.

One, it is difficult to quote specific sections of planning legislation in isolation. One section is usually qualified by another and soon the reader is floundering in the depths of section 450 (2) (iv) (b) as defined by section 727(6) (ii)(c) or some such. There is no such thing as a little bit of planning law, and to include specific statutory or policy references in any comprehensive, useful and accurate way would require a book many times the length of this one.

Second, specific references to statutes, orders, policy documents and so on have a tendency to act as stumbling blocks to the narrative. The reader soon loses sight of the forest because individual trees keep getting in the way. The purpose of this book is to provide an overview of the planning system and its procedures to enable anyone to use it.

Third, the law, orders, rules, policy documents, and so on relevant to any planning matter are best looked up in their entirety in the practitioners' handbook, *The Planning Encyclopaedia*, published by Sweet & Maxwell. Suggestions for getting access to a copy are contained in Chapter 14 'Where to go for Further Information and Advice'. Despite its daunting length (7 volumes), with a little practice anyone capable of using a telephone directory should be able to look a query about developing a listed building will be guided to the relevant sections of the 1990 Listed Buildings Act, as well as to Department of the Environment Circular 8/87, to Planning Policy Guidance (PPG) Note 1, 'General Policy and principles' and to PPG 15, 'Planning and the Historic Environment'. If the application for development to a listed building has been refused and there is to be an appeal, the appellant may also wish to look up the procedural rules governing the appeal, and so on. The index is clear and comprehensive, the commentary provided is extremely helpful, and it is updated regularly to take account of changes in law or policy.

For similar reasons I have avoided citing specific case law on any topic, because in a book of this length I doubt the reader would find reference to a correspondingly limited body of case law – itself subject to changes – particularly useful at this stage. The commentary on the individual sections of the statutes and other documents in the Encyclopaedia is regularly updated to take account of leading cases on the section or issue in point. Anyone who is concerned to find the latest case law on any topic should find this a useful starting point.

HELEN BRYAN
September 1996

Table of forms

1

Overview of the Planning System

We begin with an overview of the planning system. Any development proposal can progress through up to three stages, although the majority are resolved in the first two.

Three stages of the planning system

(1)   The local planning authority stage;
(2)   The stage where it is considered by the Secretary of State for the Environment in a public inquiry; and
(3)   The stage at which the proposal is considered by the High Court.

This is straightforward enough, but in the interests of accuracy, it is worth noting two further points about this three-stage procedure.

First it also applies to enforcement notices issued by the LPA (local planning authority) in respect of breaches of planning control (see Enforcement notices, pp. 87–89). When an enforcement notice is served by the LPA, obviously no planning application has been made. Therefore there is no planning proposal unless and until the person on whom the notice is served and who is required to take steps to remedy the breach elects to proceed to stages (2) and possibly (3). If that happens, the alleged breach of planning control is deemed by law to become an application for planning permission for the development complained of by the LPA.

Second, there are circumstances in which development proposals will effectively bypass stage (1) if the Secretary of State exercises power to 'call in' applications, i.e. to require they be referred directly to him in the first instance instead of being dealt with by the LPA. In that case there is a direct progression to stage (2).

Broadly speaking there are two circumstances in which the Secretary of State is likely to exercise the 'call in' power. One such case is when the LPA proposes to grant permission for development which departs from the development plan (see Applying the Development plan, pp. 12–13). If the LPA refuses permission and the developer appeals to the Secretary of State – stage (2) – all interested parties can put their cases for or against the proposal (see (2) Procedure at the Inquiry pp. 49–57). However, if the LPA grants permission, there is little that interested third parties can do about it other than apply for leave for judicial review (see Appeals to the High Court, pp. 77–80). By calling in the application, the Secretary of State can ensure the widest possible examination of the planning issues involved.

The second such case is when a development proposal raises planning issues of more than local importance, and the Secretary of State believes it is desirable to widen the public consultation process.

How the planning system works at each stage – the planning 'cake'

The planning 'system' is often referred to as 'planning law' or the 'law of planning', but in reality planning law is only part of the overall system which regulates development control. In reality this system has three main elements:

(i)   planning legislation,

(ii)   principles of government planning policy, and
(iii)   a process of public consultation.

These three elements are related to each other, but best understood if we consider them separately.

Imagine the planning system and its three elements as a cake with three layers, one layer for the relevant law, one for policy considerations and one for the public consultation process. Imagine that for every planning proposal, a slice of cake is cut.

We now turn to a consideration of stages (1), (2) and (3), with the piece of cake as a reminder that all three elements apply at each stage.

2

Stage (1): Planning applications

Law

In outline, the law governing stage (1) requires that an intending developer makes an application to the local planning authority for planning permission if planning permission is necessary. The law further defines when a planning application is or is not necessary, the form the application must take, how the local planning authority (the LPA) deals with applications and how the public is consulted.

When is a planning application necessary?

The main planning legislation regulating control over development is the 1990 Town and Country Planning Act. Broadly speaking, the Act provides that it is unlawful to carry out 'development' and 'new development' without planning permission unless such development or new development is exempt from the requirement. S.55 of the Act defines 'development' and 'new development' as 'the carrying out of building, engineering mining or other operations in, on, over or under land, or the making of any material change of use of any buildings or other land'.

Planning permission is required from the LPA, for most building works, for rebuilding or changes of use of an existing building unless an exemption applies. Development can be exempt in one of three ways:

(i) If the development in question comes within certain exempted categories set out in S.55, planning permission is not necessary.

(ii) If the proposal is 'development' within the meaning of S.55 it may nevertheless not require planning permission because it is 'permitted development' under the Town and Country Planning (General Permitted Development) Order 1995.

(iii) If the change of use is 'materials', it may nevertheless not require permission if it is a change to another use of the same or similar type under the 1987 Use Classes Order.

Permitted development rights

It is not always clear whether or not planning permission is required or the proposal falls within one of the exemptions. In most cases where building works or alterations are involved, it will be clear whether what is intended falls within or without the limits for 'permitted development', because the amount or size of what is permitted without permission is measurable in metres or cubic capacity.

However, the General Development Order 1995 contains provisions allowing LPAs to restrict permitted development rights in some circumstances. If the LPA has exercised their power to restrict permitted development rights, the effect is not to prohibit development altogether, but to require that planning permission be obtained in the usual way from the LPA before the development can go ahead. If permitted development rights have been restricted, development carried out without permission is unlawful.

Changes of use: when permission is necessary

'Changes of use' can also be problematic. In planning terms an intensification of an existing lawful use can amount to a 'change of use' requiring permission. An example is a proposal to turn a single dwelling house into flats. In both cases the 'use' is residential, but the proposal is an intensification of that use that amounts to a material change of use and therefore one requiring planning permission.

It can also be difficult to tell if a proposal amounts to a change of use if it is for something that is ancillary or complementary to an existing use. An example is the hotel owner who wishes to provide a bar and restaurant or leisure facilities for guests.

Sui generis use

There is a further problem which can arise in the case of changes of use which is worth mentioning, because a failure to spot something known as a 'sui generis' use or 'a use of its own kind' can lead to considerable confusion.

The 1987 Use Classes Order sets out various classes of use. Each class has a number of sub-classes of use, and a change of use within those sub-classes does not require permission. For example, Class A of the Use Classes Order permits premises used for retail sales to be used as a post office without further permission.

The question of 'sui generis' can arise in one of several ways. If the existing use is outside all the specified use classes, the existing use is probably 'sui generis' and a change of use to any other use will need planning permission. That is fairly straightforward.

Where it starts to become complicated is when an existing 'generis' use already incorporates one or more features of uses recognized by the Order, or where the development proposal is in some respects similar to the existing use but may differ in that it incorporates other uses as well.

An example is the case of the redundant police hostel. A hostel is 'sui generis' and a change of use to any other purpose will require planning permission. Assume there is a proposal to turn the police hostel into hostel accommodation for the homeless, with provision for counselling and support facilities for those with drink or drug problems. The hostel use is still 'sui generis' but a question arises as to whether the provision of counselling and support services means that the hostel is no longer purely a hostel, but is a 'residential institution' and a Class C2 use recognized by the Order and defined as 'Use for the provision of residential accommodation and care to people in need of care'.

If the change of use was simply from hostel use to hostel use, no further permission would be necessary. If there is a change of use from a 'sui generis' use (hostel) to a Class C2 use (residential institution) permission is necessary.

Whether the proposed use as a hostel for the homeless is a C2 use probably depends on the extent to which the support and counselling services are to be provided, and whether there will be a resident counsellor, warden or other support staff, etc.

This is the sort of planning issue which can quickly become bogged down in confusion, with future ramifications for everyone concerned. If the present and proposed uses are not properly identified at the outset, there is a risk that a change of use may go ahead without the necessary permission. If so, it may be open to any third parties to raise the issue of unlawful development at a later stage, and bring pressure to bear on the LPA to take enforcement action to require the change of use to cease.

Intending developers can look up the 1995 Permitted Development Order or the 1987 Use Classes Order for themselves, but in cases of doubt it is always advisable for a prospective developer to apply to the LPA under S.191 of the Act, describing the use or development proposed and asking whether it is 'lawful', i.e. may be carried out without further permission. If a developer thinks an existing use may be 'sui generis', this should be drawn to the LPA's attention.

If there is a particularly complex issue, it may be advisable to take legal advice as well.

The LPA will either issue a certificate stating that the proposed works or change of use is lawful, which means the proposal may proceed without permission, or will reject the application, which means the developer must seek planning permission.

Developers should resolve the question of whether or not permission is needed before going ahead. If development or change of use which needs planning permission is carried out without permission, that development or change of use is unlawful and in breach of planning control. The LPA may take enforcement proceedings against a breach of planning control, and force the removal or demolition of the unlawful development or the cessation of the unlawful use. This may involve the developer in considerable expense and ultimately a possible criminal prosecution, a fine and/or a prison sentence.

Advice to developers

Think ahead before making a planning application

Assuming a development proposal requires planning permission, it usually makes sense for the developer to consult the LPA before making the application to identify any potential problems in advance. If the proposal is a large or complex one, and particularly if the developer intends to go to the expense of submitting architects' plans with the application, it will save time and money to see if any elements of the proposal are likely to arouse opposition from either the LPA or local residents or interest groups. Developers should never underestimate how effective local opposition can be in blocking development proposals, and obviously it is sensible to eliminate as many potential problems as possible at the outset.

Developers will find it helpful to understand how the LPA will eventually deal with the planning application.

The LPA's approach to applications

(i) On the merits

First, the LPA must consider every application on its merits. Considering the application on its merits means that each application should be considered individually on its particular features. Each application must be looked at afresh. If you are proposing to build a seven storey neon-lit concrete car park in the middle of a conservation area consisting largely of Georgian houses, your proposal should still be considered 'on its merits' and not simply rejected out of hand (although it may well be that the application of the development plan and other material considerations lead to its rejection).

At the same time, S.70 (2) of the Act requires the LPA to have regard to the provisions of the development plan and 'all material considerations'.

(ii) Applying the development plan

The development plan is extremely important, as it is the planning blueprint regulating development in any given area. It provides for and regulates the future development of the area on the basis of the assessed needs of the inhabitants of the area, and will contain both planning objectives and the planning policies framed to achieve these objectives. For example, there may be an identified need in a given area for provision of low cost housing for single people, or policies designed to encourage development which provides jobs in areas of high unemployment.

These plans are prepared in accordance with the requirements of the act through a process of public consultation and are then formally adopted by the LPA and approved by the Secretary of State. What the development plan actually consists of depends on the size of the area in question. Every area now has, and has had for many years, an overall structure plan. The structure plan often incorporates one or more local plans as well. If the area contains conservation areas, historic buildings or green belt land, or special local features, there may be local plans with specific policies which apply only to those areas. The development plan normally contains a broad range of policies, covering topics like appropriate locations for different types of development, transport routes, standards for the size and density of new housing development, the number of parking spaces which must be provided per unit of new housing or a presumption against certain types of new development in specified areas.

London and metropolitan areas are in the process of preparing unitary development plans, to co-ordinate development in these areas. Such plans which are in the course of preparation but not yet formally adopted by the LPA or approved by the Secretary of State may still be quite important and relevant to a development proposal.

The LPA can tell developers which policies in the structure plan, local plan or emerging unitary development plan will apply to any given proposal.

Quite often these policies are couched in qualified terms, such as 'normally a policy of x will apply', or 'normally the LPA will seek to encourage y development in z location'. Developers ought to be aware of the exact wording of the applicable policies.

Developers should also appreciate that the LPA has a statutory obligation to 'seek the objectives of the structure plan' under S.1 para 8 of the Act, and that S.54A of the Act requires 'Where in making any determination under the planning Acts, regard is to be had to the development plan, the determination shall be made in accordance with the plan unless material considerations indicate otherwise.'

The starting point for intending developers should therefore be to look at any development proposal in the context of the applicable development plan policies. The LPA will have a copy and normally are extremely helpful in explaining which policies apply. However, developers should take a thorough look at the plan themselves to ensure they are familiar with all relevant policies.

(iii) Material considerations

The material considerations which the LPA must take into account by law are an almost open ended category, and will depend on the features of the proposal in question and the impact it is likely to have. If considerations are 'material' they must be planning considerations. Some examples of material considerations are whether a proposal would have the effect of preserving an historic building, meet a local need, provide some element of planning gain, the availability of alternative sites or the effect on the environment. One important category of material considerations are the representations made by local residents or interest groups, known as 'third parties'. We deal with this topic below.

Generally speaking, material considerations must relate to the development in an objective, as opposed to a subjective, way, and to some extent it is easier to identify what is not a material planning consideration.

For example, the planning system only protects private interests if there is a planning consideration, and sometimes this will depend on how the consideration is expressed. For example, if a proposed block of flats will interfere with a neighbouring householder's views, the householder who says 'I object to the loss of my views' is not making a planning objection. However, if the householder says 'The proposal will have an adverse effect on the amenity of neighbouring properties' this is a planning consideration.

The law (top layer of the cake) requires all material planning considerations be taken into account. This requirement brings the central government planning policy layer (the second layer) into the picture. Government policy is not itself law, but as a matter of practice, it is a material consideration required by law to be taken into account.

Government policy on planning and development

Broadly speaking, government policy is that development ought to go ahead, provided there are no reasons it should not. Any developer or third party will probably wish to know how this operates in practice.

Periodically, central government issues planning policy statements in the form of Department of the Environment circulars, or planning policy guidance notes about particular types of development and/or the approach which should be adopted by LPAs and developers when considering applications for particular development proposals.

For example, government policy, as well as the Town and Country Planning Act, requires LPAs to apply the policies of the development plan to any proposal.

These policy statements – the government policy element of the planning system – are not 'law' in the sense they are not statutes and have not been passed by Parliament. They also do not have the status of statutory instruments, whose future existence is provided for by a statute, which grants power to the Secretary of State to make such future regulations to give effect to that legislation, without the further need for Parliamentary consultation or approval.

Despite the fact these policy statements are not law, rather confusingly they are applied by LPAs, planning inspectors and the courts, at every stage of the planning process as if they were. These policy statements are a highly material consideration, and therefore required by S.70(2) to be taken into consideration.

The circulars and planning policy guidance notes contain a wide range of policy advice. One or more of these documents will be applicable in the case of every development proposal. For example, if the proposal concerns development in Green Belts, there is specific policy guidance concerning general restrictions on development in green belts, recognizing the special role played by green belts as an amenity containing urban sprawl, and the necessity for such development as does take place to be 'appropriate'.

Developers and third parties should be aware the LPA will take central government policy into account when determining applications, and may therefore find it helpful to consult the LPA about what the specific policy advice is and how it is applied in the area.

Public consultation

Still at the pre-application stage, we turn to a consideration of the likely effects of public consultation – the third element of the planning system – on the proposal. While there is no public consultation until a planning application is submitted, it may be sensible for a developer to anticipate what objections, if any, may be raised once the application is made and what effect this is likely to have on the outcome of the application. It is worth considering this element in advance because objections to a proposal may lead to its being turned down by either the LPA or, on appeal, the Secretary of State.

To avoid wasting money preparing development schemes which are likely to be vigorously resisted and possibly rejected, an intending developer may find it useful to consult with local residents or any local interest groups before making the application.

Surprisingly often, local residents will not object to a proposal in principle, but will object bitterly (and effectively) to particular features of the proposal, causing a proposal to be refused. If these can be identified and eliminated at the outset, it will obviously save both time and money and possibly facilitate the grant of planning permission.

Submitting the application

Application forms are available from the LPA and are self-explanatory. A fee is payable and varies depending on the application.

An intending developer does not have to own the land to apply for planning permission, but the application form specifies that if the applicant is not the freeholder, the freeholder and all parties with an interest in the land must be notified by the party applying for permission that the application is being made.

The application may be for 'outline' planning permission, leaving the question of details or 'reserved matters' – siting, design, external appearance, access and landscaping – for subsequent approval by the LPA, or for full planning permission. In the latter case all details will be submitted at the time of the application, in the form of accompanying plans and drawings.

The LPA may require further information about the proposal to make its determination.

APPLICATION FOR PLANNING PERMISSION

For Office Use Only	App. No.									

PLEASE READ THE ACCOMPANYING NOTES BEFORE COMPLETING THIS FORM

1. Name and Address of Applicant

Name ....

Address ....

....

....

....

Postcode ....

Daytime Tel. No ....

2. Name and Address of Agent *(if completed by Agent)*

Name ....

Address ....

....

....

Postcode ....

Contact Name ....

Daytime Tel. No ....

3. Full Postal Address of the Application Site

....

.... Postcode ....

4. Brief Description Proposal

A ....

....

B Total area of the application site (please specify in square metres or hectares)

C If your proposal (including change of use) exceeds 3,000 cubic metres or is more than 1,000 square metres in floor area, please tick box

5. Type of Application *(please tick ONE box)*

A Full application for a change of use only and does not involve any other works at present ☐

B Full application for a change of use and/or new building or other works ☐

C Outline application *Go to C.6* ☐

D Reserved matters application ☐ *Go to Q.7*

E Application for removal or variation of a condition ☐ *Go to Q.8*

F Application for temporary permission or renewal of a temporary permission ☐ *Go to Q.9*

6. Outline Application If you have ticked 5C above, tick relevant boxes in A below and complete B

A The following matters are reserved for future consideration:
External appearance ☐   Siting ☐   Design ☐   Means of Access ☐   Landscaping ☐

B Site Area [   ] hectares

7. Reserved Matters Applications If you have ticked 5d above, tick relevant boxes in B below

A Please state Reference Number of outline permission | App. No. | W | | / | | | | / | 0 | 0 |

B Please state which reserved matters are dealt with in this application:
External appearance ☐   Siting ☐   Design ☐   Means of Access ☐   Landscaping ☐

C Are any details required by conditions on the outline application included in this application in addition to the "reserved matters" ticked in B?   Yes or No [   ]

Please give details ....

....

PLANNING TRANSPORT AND DEVELOPMENT DEPARTMENT

Figure 1 **Planning Application Form**

8. **Application for Removal or Variation of Condition Only**

If you have ticked 5E overleaf, please give the reference no.
of permission containing conditions:

App. No. | W | | / | | | | / | |

Please state the condition nos. referred to in this application

Cond. Nos. | | | | | |

9. **Application for Temporary Permission Only**

A How long is the period of time for which temporary permission is requested?..............................

B If you have ticked 5F above and this application relates to the
renewal of temporary permission please state Ref. No. of the
current temporary permission

App. No. | W | | / | | | | / | T | P |

PLEASE COMPLETE THE FOLLOWING QUESTIONS FOR ALL APPLICATIONS

10. **ACCESS TO ROADS AND PUBLIC RIGHTS OF WAY** *(Please answer YES or NO)*

	Vehicular	Pedestrian
Will there be any new access to a public road, any alteration to an existing access to a public road, or any alteration to an existing public right of way? New	☐	☐
Alteration	☐	☐

11. **Trees, Shrubs or Hedges**

Are there any trees, shrubs or hedges in the vicinity of the proposed works?
If YES, indicate exact positions and spread on the site plans accompanying this
application and show which, if any, are to be felled, which are to be retained
and/or which will have works carried out on them.   *(Please answer YES or NO)* ☐

12. **Existing Uses**

Please state existing or, if vacant, the last use(s) of site ....

If residential state existing number of dwelling units ....

13. **Type of Development**

A Does the proposal involve any non-residential development? (including the
loss of non-residential uses) – If YES, complete Form PP2 (6 copies)   *(Please answer YES or NO)* ☐

B If the proposal involves residential development, state the number of new dwelling units proposed according to
the number of bedrooms as follows (N.B. This part does not apply to extensions to existing units)

1 Bedroom ☐	3 Bedrooms ☐	5+ Bedrooms ☐
2 Bedrooms ☐	4 Bedrooms ☐	Total ☐

C If the proposal involves any loss of residential accommodation (by demolition
or change of use), state the number of dwelling units lost ☐

14. **Drainage**

A Surface water will be disposed of to: Soakaway ☐   Surface Drains ☐   Other ☐

If other, give details ....

B Foul sewage will be disposed of to: Mains Sewer ☐   Cesspit ☐   Septic Tank ☐   Other ☐

If other, give details ....

Signed ....(Applicant/Agent) Date ....

CHECKLIST

Please tick

A 6 copies of this form, signed and dated ☐

B 6 copies of the Certificate of Ownership, signed and dated ☐

C Fee enclosed (If no fee is enclosed, please give reason below) ☐

....

D 6 copies of scaled plans including: ☐

(i) the location plan with application site outlined in red. ☐

(ii) the block/layout plan showing the position of adjoining land and buildings ☐

(iii) floor plans and elevations ☐

Figure 1 Planning Application Form (Cont'd)

In cases where a large development proposal is likely to have a significant impact on the local environment, the developer may be required to provide an environmental impact assessment before the LPA will consider the application (see Chapter 11).

A planning application may be made for development which has already been carried out.

If development has taken place without permission, or in accordance with a temporary permission or without complying with a condition attached to a previous grant of planning permission, a planning application can be made to legitimize what is otherwise unlawful development.

Planning officer

An officer in the planning department will be assigned to each application. Normally the developer will liaise with that officer if any questions arise or consultation is necessary.

The planning officer will visit the site of the proposed development, gauge the likely impact and consider how the policies of the development plan apply to the proposal. The planning officer will then prepare a formal report on the proposal for the planning committee or subcommittee which is composed of elected council members.

To return to the top layer of the planning system cake, once an application is submitted by the developer, the law requires the LPA to advertise the application in the press and to post a site notice stating that a planning application has been made. The notice in the press and at the site will state what the application is for and where the application and any plans or supporting documents are available for public inspection. Normally this will be at the LPA offices during working hours. The notices will state that anyone wishing to make representations about the proposal must do so to the planning department or the planning officer named within three weeks of the date of the notice.

While LPAs are not required by law to notify individual local residents in the immediate vicinity of the application site, nevertheless in practice many do so. However, anyone who has not been notified but believes an application may have been made, can ask to inspect the LPA's planning register, on which all applications for planning permission are recorded.

The third element of the planning system – public consultation – now becomes relevant. Parties other than the developer and the LPA are known as 'third parties'. Any third party potentially affected by the development may make representations to the LPA about the application. The LPA must take these representations into account as material considerations provided they are planning considerations.

Public consultation at stage (1) of the planning system

This will be done by letter to the planning department, or to the planning officer assigned to the application. Anyone can write a letter, but before doing so is strongly advised to go and see the application and any plans or supporting documents. Third parties should also ask the planning officer what development plan policies apply, and may wish to look at the development plan themselves.

Letters making representations

These should refer to the application number and the address of the site. It is helpful if the writer identifies him or herself and in what capacity he or she is affected by the proposal, i.e. as neighbours, someone whose livelihood may be adversely affected, a member of a local amenity group or association, etc. If speaking on behalf of an organization – for example a residents' association or a local amenity society – indicate how many people your group represents.

While all letters will be taken into account, the same photocopied form letter sent by many people is best avoided. Individually worded letters are better. Alternatively, a number of people may wish to add their signatures to a single letter.

A copy of any letters or representations should be sent to the third party's local councillors and the chairman of the planning committee.

Third party representations are usually thought to be objections. While this is often true, sometimes individuals or organizations will wish to make representations of support.

In other cases, third parties may simply wish to recommend modifications. For example, neighbours may say they object to a new block of flats which will be twice the size of neighbouring buildings but would not object to a modified scheme in keeping with the neighbourhood, set further back in the site or which eliminated windows overlooking neighbouring properties.

It is always sensible for third parties to consider thoroughly what is actually involved in the proposal and whether it can be acceptably modified. The reason for this statement is that if one planning application for a site is turned down, another is likely to follow in future. In some cases, third parties may prefer to see a proposal, suitably amended, go ahead rather than fight the battle afresh time after time.

When making representations, it is sensible for third parties to check what development plan policies apply and to refer to them when writing to the LPA about the proposal. As representations should always be couched in ' planning terms' to be taken into account as material considerations. Third parties may find the wording of the policies and objectives of the development plan a useful guide.

If there are any special considerations – for example, if the application concerns development to an historic building, or in a conservation area or green belt – it makes sense to relate the representations to these considerations.

It is sometimes the case that third parties will notice a particular aspect of the proposal which the planning officer has not appreciated, but which ought to be mentioned in the report to the planning committee. If anyone suspects this is the case, it is possible to request to meet the planning officer to indicate what these aspects might be. The planning officer is not obliged to meet third parties, but in practice most people find planning officers approachable and interested in all possible aspects of the development.

Third parties and the press

Third parties will often find the local press an important ally in planning matters. Normally a planning proposal which affects the locality is newsworthy, and if there are particular features or a human interest angle, so much the better. Particularly interesting planning stories may be picked up by the national press.

Rightly or wrongly, third parties sometimes feel there is little point making representations because they will have little or no effect on the ultimate decision. Raising planning issues in the press is an effective way of 'reinforcing' representations made to the planning department and local councillors. Councillors who make the ultimate decision on the planning application are elected by local residents and may be even more responsive to any views expressed by their electorate if these are covered in the media. Raising the matter in the press is one of the best and most effective ways of ensuring that public consultation is indeed 'public'.

Amending the application

In the course of the public consultation process and the preparation of the officer's report, it may become apparent to the developer that particular aspects of the application conflict with development plan policy and/or arouse local opposition, to such an extent that the proposal is likely to be refused. If so, this will leave the developer with the choice of going on to the next stage of the process – an appeal to the Secretary of State and a public planning inquiry – abandoning the proposal or making a fresh and possibly amended application in the future.

However, is always possible to amend the current application at any time if it appears desirable to do so because an amended scheme may be more likely to be approved.

LPA's determination of the application

The LPA should determine the application within eight weeks. If they fail to do so, the developer has a right of appeal to the Secretary of State for non-determination in much the same way as there is a right of appeal against the LPA's refusal of planning permission (see Chapter 3, Stage (2) Appeals and Public Planning Inquiries.

Elected councillors who are members of the planning committee or subcommittee will determine the application. As we have already seen, the threefold exercise they must perform is to:

(i)   consider the application on its merits,
(ii) apply the development plan, and
(iii) take into account all material considerations, including the representations of third parties.

The planning officer's report recommending the appropriate course for the LPA to take will be prepared with this exercise in mind, and will be taken into account by the members.

However, it is not unusual for the planning officer to take the view that permission ought to be granted, but to find the local councillors override that view and refuse, or vice versa. When this happens it is often a result of an effective third party campaign to lobby councillors for a particular result, and the councillors are, not surprisingly, responding to the views of their constituents. The importance of the 'public consultation' element of the planning system should never be underestimated.

It should be possible to attend the planning committee meeting determining the application, and in some cases to make brief representations to the committee at the time. However, if the committee are likely to refuse the application, there will be no need to hear from objectors, or if likely to approve, no need to hear from the developer or supporters. Whether anything further can usefully be said at the meeting will depend on the particular proposal and the strength of third party views.

Anyone wishing to know when a particular application is being dealt with or whether they may attend or speak should contact the clerk to the planning committee at the LPA.

Applications an LPA may refuse to determine

If within two years of the application being received, an application for the same or similar development on the same or similar land has been refused on appeal to the Secretary of State (at stage (2)), the LPA may decline to determine the application if there has been no change in the development plan and the material considerations remain the same.

The LPA has discretion whether or not to exercise their power to refuse. Bearing this in mind, a developer may wish to ascertain the planning history of a site before incurring expense on plans, and professional advice prior to making an application, and consult the LPA as to whether it is likely to refuse determination.

The LPA's decision

The LPA can determine the planning application in one of three ways:

(i)   by granting planning permission,
(ii)   by refusing planning permission, or
(iii)   by granting planning permission subject to conditions.

Conditions

These may be attached to the grant of planning permission if appropriate and the proposal could not go ahead otherwise. Sometimes these conditions will be imposed in response to representations made by third parties.

Conditions must have certain characteristics: they must relate to the development in question, be necessary to enable the development to proceed, be relevant to planning, precise, reasonable and capable of enforcement.

If conditional planning permission is granted, the development will only be lawful if the conditions are complied with. If a developer feels the conditions imposed do not meet the criteria – for example, if meeting them would require unreasonable levels of expenditure – there is a right of appeal to the Secretary of State, who will order a planning inquiry to determine whether the conditions ought to be removed.

An applicant who is refused planning permission may appeal to the Secretary of State, as may a developer whose application has not been determined within eight weeks.

If the LPA has notified the applicant that it has declined

to determine the application because there has been a similar application refused on appeal within two years, the developer cannot appeal to the Secretary of State, and the only remedy available is to apply for leave for judicial review of the LPA's decision to refuse to determine the application.

If the application approved was an outline application, a further application must be made for specific approval of reserved matters (siting, design, external appearance, access and land-scaping, etc.).

The LPA will notify the developer of their determination of the application. If the application was approved subject to conditions, the reasons for imposing those conditions will be specified. If the application was refused, the decision letter will specify the reasons why.

If the application was approved, normally it will be subject to a standard condition that the permission must be implemented – some step taken to begin the development approved – within five years. If the permission is not implemented or begun within five years, it lapses and a fresh permission must be applied for to carry out the development.

Planning obligations

Planning obligations, as distinct from planning conditions, can be used as a means of facilitating planning permission by using them to achieve a particular planning objective in relation to the development proposed. This can be done through a unilateral undertaking given by the developer, or by mutual agreement between the developer and the LPA.

A planning obligation may do a number of things. It may restrict the development or use of land in a particular way, require the developer to carry out certain activities or operations on or under the land, require that the land be put to a specific use, or require payment of sums of money to the LPA.

A planning obligation binds not only the present owner of the land who gives the undertaking or enters into an agreement with the LPA, it binds subsequent purchasers of the land as well.

An example of circumstances in which a planning obligation

might be appropriate is the case of a developer proposing to build a large shopping complex on vacant inner city land suitable for housing, when the development plan provides for the increased provision of low-cost housing. In the circumstances, a developer's willingness to enter into a planning obligation to provide an element of low-cost housing as part of the overall development might overcome any reluctance or objections on planning grounds on the part of the LPA.

Generally a planning obligation is only appropriate for on-site obligations. It must be executed by deed and is registerable as a local land charge. It is enforceable by the LPA against the developer and the developer's successors in title. If the developer proposing to build the shopping complex enters into a planning obligation to build some low cost housing as well, that obligation would bind any subsequent purchaser of the site, even if the site were sold on by the developer without having built the shopping complex.

Unlike a condition, which can be removed by the Secretary of State on appeal, a planning obligation can only be cancelled by the Lands Tribunal.

Planning obligations are a less flexible way of achieving a particular planning result, and for this reason government policy favours the use of conditions over planning obligations, where possible.

The developer's right of appeal to Secretary of State

The developer may appeal to the Secretary of State against a refusal of planning permission, including a refusal of permission for reserved matters following an outline application approved by the LPA. There is also a right of appeal against the LPA's decision to grant permission subject to conditions.

Third parties – no right of appeal to Secretary of State

Third parties cannot appeal to the Secretary of State if they are dissatisfied with the LPA's decision to grant planning permission. The only course of action open to third parties is judicial review of the LPA's decision in the High Court.

This is a two stage process. There is a preliminary hearing to apply to the court for leave for judicial review. If leave is granted, a full judicial review hearing takes place.

The grounds on which an action for judicial review may be brought are that the LPA has acted outside its powers in granting permission. Judicial review is potentially costly in that in court actions the loser must generally bear the winner's costs in addition to the costs incurred by the losing side.

Temporary development

Some forms of temporary development and use are permitted under the Permitted Development Order. For example, a market may be held or motorcycle racing may take place without planning permission for the activity or any movable structures which may be erected for the duration of the activity, provided it is not for more than 14 days in the year.

Otherwise, a wide variety of uses may take place for up to 28 days a year without permission, subject to certain restrictions. Anyone who believes planning permission is not necessary is still advised to consult the LPA to verify the position.

Local residents or anyone who is concerned by the activity taking place may also contact the LPA with any queries as to whether the activity is permitted under the order or not. It is sometimes the case that the LPA is unaware of a possibly unauthorized use until local residents' complaints bring it to their attention. Once this happens, the LPA normally investigate and can initiate enforcement proceedings if appropriate.

In addition, it is sometimes the case that a permission is granted on a temporary basis, because it is subject to a condition limiting the life of the permission. This is sometimes done to allow a developer an opportunity to make alternative arrangements for the relocation of the development, or if the LPA feels it would be appropriate to give the development a trial run.

If permission is temporary because of a time limiting condition, the developer can always apply for removal of the condition. If the LPA refuse, there is a right of appeal to the Secretary of State.

Checklist for planning application

What developers should do:

- Confirm with the LPA whether planning permission is required, if in doubt:
- Before making the application
  - consult the LPA
  - ask which development plan policies apply
  - ask what government policy advice applies and try to assess potential objections
  - consult local residents or potential third party objectors
  - see if any third parties are in favour of development proposal
- On making application
  - fill out an application form
  - pay the fee
  - ensure all parties with an interest in the land have been served with the correct notice of intended development
  - submit plans and drawings if appropriate
  - discuss amendments to proposal with LPA if appropriate

What third parties should do:

- upon learning or suspecting a planning application has been submitted:
  - check the planning register if they believe an

application has been submitted but they have not seen a site notice or notice in the local press
- inspect the application and any supporting plans on display
- be clear about what is proposed
- ask the LPA what development plan policies apply
- ask the LPA what government policies apply
- look in the register and/or ask the LPA whether there have been similar development proposals in the area recently approved or refused by the LPA
- write letters expressing any views about the proposal to the planning department within three weeks

● When writing letters:

- cite the application reference number
- identify the writer's proximity to or interest in the proposal, and if writing as the representative of a group, state how many people the group represents
- remember to make representations in planning terms
- if the proposal would be acceptable if modified, say what modifications or amendments would be appropriate
- state what development plan and/or government policy applies or ought to apply
- request to be informed of the LPA's decision
- send copies of letters to local councillors and the chairman of the planning committee

● Contact the local press
● Contact the clerk to the planning committee and ask if it is possible to attend when the committee consider the application and if third parties may make brief representations at that meeting

3

Stage (2) of the Planning System: Appeals and Public Planning Inquiries: General Information

Moving on to consider how appeals arise and are dealt with, it may help to recall the slice of planning cake as a reminder that the three elements of the planning system – law, government policy and public consultation – apply at the appeal stage.

When a planning inquiry is held

A public planning inquiry can be held in a number of circumstances. In most cases these will be held because a developer has appealed to the Secretary of State, for example:

- if the LPA refuses planning permission the developer may appeal to the Secretary of State for the Environment to hold a public inquiry to determine the application.
- if planning permission has been granted subject to conditions which the developer believes are unreasonable, or will prevent the development going ahead, or which otherwise do not conform to the requirements for conditions, the developer may appeal to the Secretary of State for the removal of the condition. A public inquiry will be held to determine whether the condition should be removed.
- if the LPA has not determined the application within the eight-week period prescribed by law, the Secretary of State

will order a public inquiry to determine the application.

- if the LPA has refused an application for approval of reserved matters, following approval of an outline application.
- if the LPA has taken enforcement action against a breach of planning control (see Enforcement action, page xxx) the party served with the notice and required to remedy the breach may appeal to the Secretary of State, who will order a public inquiry to determine the validity of the enforcement notice. If the result is to declare the notice invalid, the LPA cannot require the removal of the development or cessation of the use which was subject of the notice.
- if the LPA has refused listed building or conservation area consent (see Chapter 9).
- if the Secretary of State has 'called in' an application to determine, an applicant may request a public inquiry to examine the issues raised by the development. A public inquiry held for this reason is not the result of an appeal.

Likewise, most major development proposals, such as motorways, airports, nuclear power installations, etc., will go straight to the public inquiry stage.

How and when an appeal must be made in respect of a planning application

A developer who wishes to appeal against a refusal of permission or the grant of conditional planning permission must do so within six months of the LPA's decision. In the case of a failure to determine the application, the appeal must be lodged within six months after the expiry of the eight-week determination period. A notice of appeal must be sent to the Department of the Environment within that time.

The notice of appeal form can be obtained from:

The Secretary of State for the Environment
Tollgate House
Houlton Street
Bristol BS2 9DJ

The Planning Inspectorate

An Executive Agency in the Department of the Environment and the Welsh Office

PLANNING APPEAL

FOR OFFICIAL USE ONLY
Date received

The appeal must reach the Inspectorate within 6 months of the date of the Notice of the Local
Planning Authority's Decision, or within 6 months of the date by which they should have decided the application.

A. INFORMATION ABOUT THE APPELLANT(S)

Full Name: ....

Address: ....

....

Postcode: .... Reference: ....
Failure to provide the postcode may cause delay in processing your appeal.

Daytime Telephone No: .... Fax No: ....

Agent's Name (if any): ....

Agent's Address: ....

....

Postcode: .... Reference: ....
Failure to provide the postcode may cause delay in processing your appeal.

Daytime Telephone No: .... Fax No: ....

B. DETAILS OF THE APPEAL

Name of the Local Planning Authority (LPA):

Description of the Development:

Address of the Site:	National Grid Reference (see key on OS map for Instructions). Grid Letters: Grid Numbers eg TQ:298407
Postcode: *Failure to provide the postcode may cause delay in processing your appeal.*	
Date and LPA reference number of the application you made and which is now the subject of this appeal:	Date of LPA Notice of Decision (if any):

Are there any outstanding appeals for this site eg Enforcement, Lawful Development Certificate etc? If so please give

details and any DOE reference number here:...

....

1

(Rev 1996)

Figure 2 Notice of appeal form (Crown copyright reproduced with the permission of the Controller of HMSO)

C. REASON FOR THE APPEAL

THIS APPEAL IS AGAINST the decision of the LPA:-   (* Delete as appropriate)   (✔)

1. to *refuse/grant subject to conditions, planning permission for the development described in Section B.

2. to *refuse/grant subject to conditions, approval of the matters reserved under an outline planning permission.

3. to refuse to approve any matter (other than those mentioned in 2 above) required by a condition on a planning permission.

Or the failure of the LPA:-
4. to give notice of their decision within the appropriate period on an application for permission or approval.

D. CHOICE OF PROCEDURE

CHOOSE ONE OF THE FOLLOWING TYPES OF PROCEDURE - These are described fully in the booklet 'Planning Appeals - A Guide' which accompanied this form.

1. WRITTEN REPRESENTATIONS

If you have chosen the written representations procedure, please tick if the whole site can clearly be seen from a road or other public land. (An unaccompanied site visit will be arranged if the Inspector can adequately view the site from public land.)

2. LOCAL INQUIRY Please give reasons why an inquiry is necessary ....

....

3. HEARING Although you may prefer a hearing, the LPA need to agree to this procedure and the Inspectorate must consider your appeal suitable.

E. ESSENTIAL SUPPORTING DOCUMENTS

A copy of each of the following should be enclosed with this form.

1. The application submitted to the LPA;

2. The site ownership details (Article 7 certificate) submitted to the LPA at application stage;

3. Plans, drawings and documents forming part of the application submitted to the LPA;

4. The LPA's decision notice (if any);

5. Other relevant correspondence with the LPA;

6. A plan showing the site in red, in relation to two named roads (preferably on an extract from the relevant 1:10,000 OS map). (Failure to submit this can delay your appeal).

Copies of the following should also be enclosed, if appropriate:

7. If the appeal concerns reserved matters, the relevant outline application, plans submitted and the permission;

8. Any plans, drawings and documents sent to the LPA but which do not form part of the submitted application (eg drawings for illustrative purposes);

9. Additional plans or drawings relating to the application but not previously seen by the LPA. Please number them clearly and list the numbers here:..

2

Figure 2 Notice of appeal form (Continued)

F.   APPEAL SITE OWNERSHIP DETAILS

IMPORTANT: THE ACCOMPANYING NOTES SHOULD BE READ BEFORE THE APPROPRIATE
CERTIFICATE IS COMPLETED. CERTIFICATES A AND B ARE GIVEN BELOW. IF NEEDED, CERTIFICATES C
AND D ARE ATTACHED TO THE GUIDANCE NOTES.

<u>SITE OWNERSHIP CERTIFICATES</u>

PLEASE DELETE INAPPROPRIATE WORDING WHERE INDICATED (*) AND STRIKE OUT INAPPLICABLE
CERTIFICATE

CERTIFICATE A

I certify that:
> On the day 21 days before the date of this appeal nobody, except the appellant, was the owner (see Note (i) of the
> guidance notes) of any part of the land to which the appeal relates.

OR

CERTIFICATE B

I certify that:
> I have/the appellant has *given the requisite notice to everyone else who, on the day 21 days before the date of this
> appeal, was the owner (see Note (i) of the guidance notes) of any part of the land to which the appeal relates, as
> listed below.

Owner's Name	Address at which notice was served	Date on which notice was served

I further certify that:

<u>AGRICULTURAL HOLDINGS CERTIFICATE</u> (TO BE COMPLETED IN ALL CASES WHERE A, B, C OR D
OWNERSHIP CERTIFICATE HAS BEEN COMPLETED)

**   None of the land to which the appeal relates is, or is part of, an agricultural holding.

OR

**   I have/the appellant has *given the requisite notice to every person other than my/him/her* self who, on the day
21 days before the date of the appeal, was a tenant of an agricultural holding on all or part of the land to which
the appeal relates, as follows:

Tenant's Name	Address at which notice was served	Date on which notice was served

* **Delete as appropriate. If the appellant is the <u>sole</u> agricultural tenant the first alternative should be deleted and
"not applicable" should be inserted below the second alternative.**

Signed .... (on behalf of) ....

Name (in capitals) .... Date ....

3

Figure 2 Notice of appeal form (*Continued*)

G. GROUNDS OF APPEAL If the written procedure is requested, the appellant's FULL STATEMENT OF CASE MUST be made - otherwise the appeal may be invalid. If the written procedure has not been requested, a brief outline of the appellant's case should be made here.

Continue on a separate sheet if necessary

PLEASE SIGN BELOW

I confirm that a copy of this appeal form and any supporting documents relating to the application not previously sent to the LPA has been sent to them. I undertake that any future documents submitted in connection with this appeal will also be copied to the local planning authority at the same time.

Signed .... (on behalf of) ....

Name (in capitals) .... Date ....

CHECKLIST - Please check this list thoroughly to avoid delay in the processing of your appeal.

- This form signed and fully completed.
- Any relevant documents listed at Section E enclosed.
- Full grounds of appeal/outline of case set out at Section G.
- Relevant ownership certificate A, B, C or D completed and signed.
- Agricultural Holdings Certificate completed and signed.

◆ 1ST COPY: Send one copy of the appeal form with all the supporting documents to:
 The Planning Inspectorate
 Appeals Registry
 Tollgate House
 Houlton Street
 BRISTOL
 BS2 9DJ

◆ 2ND COPY: Send one copy to the LPA, at the address from which the decision on the application (or any acknowledgements, etc) was received, enclosing any supporting documents not previously submitted to them as part of the application.

◆ 3RD COPY: For you to keep

4

Figure 2 Notice of appeal form (Continued)

The form must be completed and sent back with the required accompanying documents within the six-month time period. The documents which must accompany the form are:

- a copy of the original application to the LPA
- copies of any plans or drawings sent to the LPA in support of the application
- any plans or drawings relating to the application which the developer did not submit to the LPA
- if the developer is not the owner of the land, copies of notices sent to anyone else having a legal interest in the land
- copies of any correspondence between the developer and the LPA about the application
- a copy of the LPA's decision or determination (if any)
- if the developer is appealing against the refusal of permission for reserved matters, a copy of the application for outline permission and any plans must be submitted, together with a copy of the outline permission granted by the LPA.

The developer who is appealing is now known as the 'appellant'. The appellant must serve a copy of the notice of appeal on the LPA as soon as reasonably practicable. The appellant must also furnish the LPA with copies of any plans or drawings or other documents in respect of the development which the LPA has not already been sent.

A failure to determine the application is treated like a decision to refuse permission unless the LPA has served a notice on the developer saying it is exercising its power not to determine the application.

In cases where the LPA has simply failed to determine the application, it is often the case that the developer will be furnished with a copy of the reasons why the application would have been refused, had the LPA determined it. If so, the appellant will know what objections the LPA will raise in the course of a public inquiry.

The DOE will make all arrangements for the inquiry, appointing an inspector to hear the appeal, fixing a date and booking a venue. An inspector will be appointed to hear the evidence and, in most cases, determine the appeal. In some cases raising complex planning issues, or issues of more than local significance, however, the inspector will hear the evidence and make a report to the Secretary of State who will make the ultimate decision.

The inspector determining the appeal or reporting on it to the Secretary of State essentially 'stands in the shoes' of the LPA and performs the same exercise the LPA performs when considering the application when made to it. This means that like the LPA, the inspector will have regard to the provisions of the development plan and all material considerations.

The form of the inquiry

There are three forms an appeal can take:

(ii)   by way of written representations,
(ii)   by way of an informal 'hearing' and
(iii)   by way of a full hearing in public.

(i) Written representations

The majority of appeals take place by the written representations method. In such cases the appellant and the LPA put forward their cases in writing, and each is given a chance to comment on the other's cases. The element of public consultation is introduced because all third parties who made representations must be notified by the LPA. All these third parties can then make written representations to the inspector.

The notice of appeal asks the appellant to note whether they are prepared for the appeal to be dealt with by way of written representations. Both the appellant and the LPA must agree to the written representation procedure. If either party wishes to have the matter heard in public before a planning inspector, the Secretary of State will order a full public inquiry, with the exception of cases in which a hearing is ordered (see Hearings, below).

The obvious advantage of the written representation procedure is that the appellant can obtain the written opinion of any professionals, such as architects, surveyors or planning consultants, upon whose evidence the appellant will rely. The cost of expert opinions in writing is far less than paying the same experts to attend a planning inquiry to give evidence at a daily rate.

Appellants are entitled by law to elect the form of inquiry they believe is most appropriate, and the choice of written representations over a public inquiry, or vice versa, will not affect the inspector's decision.

(ii) Hearings

In cases where either the appellant or the LPA or both have indicated a preference for an inquiry in public, if the Secretary of State thinks it appropriate, the parties may be given the option of a 'hearing', a sort of informal public inquiry.

A hearing is suitable in cases where the proposed development is small scale, there are no complex planning issues involved and there is minimal third party interest. The appellant and LPA appear in person, but there is less need for formal representation by professionals – barristers, solicitors or planning consultants – because the parties do not cross examine each other's evidence. The procedure is more relaxed and less formal than in a public inquiry.

The advantage of the hearing procedure is that in appropriate cases it can save time and money, and enable a decision on the appeal to be made relatively quickly. Both the appellant and the LPA must agree to proceed by way of a hearing.

(iii) Public planning inquiries

A full public planning inquiry is held in a public venue and is open to the public, including the press. The proceedings are conducted with a certain formality, although the actual procedure itself is fairly straightforward. Evidence is given orally, by the reading of written statements which have been prepared and exchanged by the parties prior to the inquiry.

After reading a statement, the witness may be cross examined on the evidence given by some or all of the other parties. With some exceptions as provided by law, third parties do not have a legal entitlement to present a case but almost invariably are permitted to do so by inspectors.

It is always open to the appellant and the LPA to elect a full public inquiry, and neither party will be penalized in any way for exercising this right. If the proposal has generated considerable third party interest, and/or is large and/or the planning issues complex, it is likely the LPA, if not the appellant, will elect a public inquiry as the most appropriate method of hearing the appeal.

The public consultation element

Public consultation is at the heart of the planning system, which has been designed to ensure development will be permitted only after all those affected have been given a chance to have their say. In the previous chapters we have seen that the law requires the LPA to notify the public, by means of a site notice and an advertisement in the local press, in order to allow any third party interested in (affected by) the proposed development to express a view to the LPA. The law requires that the result of this public consultation process be taken into account in determining the planning application.

The same principle applies in relation to planning appeals. The LPA is required by law to post a notice of the forthcoming appeal at the development site and in the local press to enable any third parties – who may or may not have written letters about the planning application – to make representations in respect of the appeal.

The public consultation element in public inquiries at stage (ii) of the planning system is often more visible than in stage (i), in that third parties have an opportunity to 'go public' with the points they wish to make. Many people find it more satisfactory to have a say in public, and rightly or wrongly believe it a more effective method of public consultation. More importantly, a full public inquiry allows for all the evidence put forward by all parties to be tested by public cross examination.

There is no set format for a pre-inquiry statement, but it should include certain information detailing the appeal, the site, the planning issues and the documents on which the party proposes to rely. On page 41 is a typical example of a pre-inquiry statement.

Figure 3 – Rule 6 pre-inquiry statement – example

Pre-inquiry statement of: _____

                                             (the party making it)

Name of the LPA: _____

Town and Country Planning (Inquiries Procedure Rules) 1988

Site: _____

                    (Address of the appeal site)

Appellant: _____

                    (Name of appellant)

Subject of inquiry: _____

                    (Description of proposed
                      development,
                    i.e. 'Application for........')

Site and surroundings: _____

                    (Description of site and any
                special features, i.e. proximity to
                  conservation area, etc.)

Planning history of site: _____

                    (If relevant)

The planning issues which arise: _____

                    (Summary of the case the
                  party is making)

1. _____

2. _____

3. _____

List of documents (including maps, plans, photographs, expert reports, DoE circulars and development plan policies, etc. on which the party proposes to rely)

The inspector was stunned by the length of the submission

4

Planning Inquiries

Although all three elements of the planning system apply in stage (1), government policy and public consultation assume a more prominent – though no more important – role at stage (2). This is a particularly important consideration for the non-specialist involved in a public planning inquiry, either as the appellant or as a third party.

In outline, the three elements feature at the inquiry stage as follows:

- Planning law governs how and when an appeal may be made against a decision of an LPA, what the procedure is, and the options available as to the form the appeal takes. The law also prescribes how the LPA must inform the public to enable public consultation at stage (ii). It also governs whether a planning inspector determines the appeal or reports to the Secretary of State, and provides for the procedural rules of the inquiry. The law requires the inspector (or the Secretary of State) to perform the same exercise required of the LPA when determining the appeal, i.e. to have regard to the development plan and all material considerations.

- Government policy is one of the most material of material considerations. Although it is not itself law, in practice it is nearly always emphasized at length at the planning inquiry stage. It assumes additional importance at the planning inquiry stage because, in addition to general policy guidelines about the development in question,

government policy also concerns the application of development plan policies. These development plan policies and their application will inevitably be central to the planning issues involved in the appeal.
- Public consultation will be a more visible element at a public inquiry, both because the public may attend to hear the appeal and because third parties may elect to publicly participate as formal parties to the inquiry.

Inquiry Procedure

The procedure for appeals by way of written representations is set out in the Town and Country Planning (Appeals) (Written Representations Procedure) Regulations, 1987.

The procedure for appeals determined by way of informal hearings is set out in a code of practice in Annex 2 of DoE Circular 10/88.

The procedure at a public planning inquiry is governed by the Town and Country Planning (Inquiries Procedure) Rules 1992 (Statutory Instrument 1992 No. 2038) if the inquiry will be determined by the Secretary of State, and the Town and Country Planning Appeals (Determination by Inspectors) (Inquiries Procedure) Rules 1992 (Statutory Instrument 1992 No. 2039) if the inspector will determine the appeal.

An appellant or third party making a formal appearance in person at an inquiry may find it helpful to obtain a copy of whichever rules apply from:

HMSO
49 High Holborn
London WC1V 6HB

or see Chapter 14, Where to go for further information and advice.

Although this chapter deals specifically with public planning inquiries, the procedure for most public inquiries is very similar, and will be subject to specific rules which can be obtained from HMSO if required.

The relevant rules are designed to ensure that the inquiry procedure is as efficient and effective as possible. Rules governing planning inquiries provide for what happens before, during and after the inquiry as follows:

(i) Pre-inquiry procedure

Public inquiries are held at public expense, and it is desirable for all parties involved to concentrate their minds on the planning issues which arise in the appeal, in order that time is not taken up unnecessarily with extraneous matters. For this reason the rules provide for an exchange of information between all the parties prior to the inquiry. This enables everyone to see the extent to which there is agreement and on what issues differences remain between them. A pre-inquiry exchange of information and proofs of evidence often reveals that parties do not dispute facts or issues A, B and C, but differ widely on X and Y. If so, there is no point taking up inquiry time with A, B and C and the appeal can concentrate on X and Y.

Following an appellant's notice of appeal, the Secretary of State for the Environment notifies both the appellant and the LPA that a public inquiry is to be held. The date of this notice is known as 'the relevant dàte' and the time limits for pre-inquiry service of information are measured from 'the relevant date'.

(ii) 'Rule 6 statements'

Both sets of rules contain the same provision at Rule 6 requiring the LPA and the appellant to serve outline statements of their cases on each other and on the Secretary of State. These are known (for obvious reasons) as Rule 6 statements. These outline statements of case do not have to be long, but they should specify all the planning issues each party intends to address in the inquiry, and be accompanied by a list of all relevant documents, including maps, plans, drawings and photographs which will be relied on.

It is important these statements are complete, because all parties to an inquiry should avoid raising new issues at the last minute.

(iii) Third parties and Rule 6 statements

Third parties – other than statutory bodies who may have an interest in the appeal proposal and thus a statutory right to appear – do not have a legal right to put in a formal appearance and present a case at a public inquiry. However, under the rules, non-statutory third parties may inform the Secretary of State that they wish to make a formal appearance and to be heard at the inquiry. If so they may serve their own Rule 6 statement on the Secretary of State. If they chose to do so, they should send a copy to the appellant and the LPA.

However, any third party who has indicated to the DoE an intention or wish to be heard at the inquiry is not automatically required by the rules to serve a Rule 6 statement unless specifically requested to do so by the Secretary of State.

Instead of, or sometimes in addition to, appearing at the inquiry, third parties may make written representations of any length to the Secretary of State about the appeal proposal, just as they make written representations to the LPA regarding a planning application. These letters will be taken into account even if the writer does not wish to say anything at the inquiry.

If a third party notifies the DoE of an intention or wish to be heard at the inquiry but does not serve a Rule 6 statement, the Secretary of State will probably not require one unless there are grounds to believe that third party is likely to raise substantive planning issues or calling substantial evidence. If so it would be desirable for the appellant and/or the LPA to be aware of the third party's case in advance through the formal serving of a Rule 6 statement.

If a third party Rule 6 statement is served on the DoE, copies must be sent to the LPA and appellant. Any third party Rule 6 statement must be accompanied by a list of any documents which will be referred to or relied upon at the inquiry. If third parties propose to introduce technical issues or evidence – such as structural engineers' reports or evidence from traffic specialists – the Rule 6 statement needs to make this clear. All parties are entitled to know what the case is they have to meet, and are entitled to time to obtain specialist evidence in rebuttal.

Once the Secretary of State has received all the relevant Rule 6 statements, he or she may require the parties to provide other information.

Aside from enabling the various parties to the inquiry, the DoE and the inspector to identify in advance what planning issues arise in the appeal, the serving of pre-inquiry statements enables the DoE, who must make suitable arrangements for the inquiry, to estimate how long the inquiry is likely to last and how large a venue needs to be booked.

It is important that no party to the inquiry needs to feel rushed in presenting a case because time was underestimated, or crowded tight in a venue which is too small. It is also important to avoid, if possible, the necessity for adjourning a part-heard inquiry to a later date.

The LPA must make available for public inspection copies of all Rule 6 statements and the documents which accompany them. The notice of appeal which the LPA is required to ensure appeals in the local press and at the appeal site will specify when and where these statements and documents can be seen. LPAs should allow members of the public to make copies of these documents where it is practicable to afford facilities for doing so.

(iv) Pre-inquiry meeting

In particularly important inquiries raising complex planning issues or concerning major development proposals, the inspector may feel it is appropriate to hold a pre-inquiry meeting to determine a timetable for the presentation of evidence.

(v) Pre-inquiry serving of proofs of evidence and summaries

Evidence at inquiries is given orally by reading from prepared written proofs. In the bad old days up until a few years ago, no one had sight of the other side's proofs until copies were handed round as the witness settled into the witness chair. This practice could be nerve-racking for advocates or indeed any of the other parties who had to prepare a cross examination at speed as the witness was reading.

The law has changed in two respects which makes dealing with the other side's evidence much easier. First, unless the inspector has substituted some other timetable, the rules require anyone proposing to give or call evidence at an inquiry to supply a copy of the full proof of evidence to the inspector not later than three weeks before the inquiry is due to begin. If the proof is longer than 1500 words, a summary must be provided as well. Unfortunately the three-week limit is not always observed, but it is probably fair to say that an inspector will not only be unimpressed at receiving proofs at the last minute, but irritated as well. The inspector is likely to be very annoyed if summaries are not provided. Late arrival of proofs may have costs implications as well (see Costs, pp. 54–57).

The appellant and the LPA must serve copies of their proofs and summaries and supporting documents on the inspector, each other, and any statutory body interested in the appeal proposal.

On a strict interpretation of the rules, non-statutory third parties proposing to give evidence should also serve a proof and summary on the inspector, the LPA and the appellant. However, in practice whether it is necessary to do so seems to be a matter of degree.

If a third party – for example, a local residents' association – wants to make representations at a one-day inquiry about the impact of a neighbour's kitchen extension on the amenity of the neighbourhood, it is probably not necessary to furnish the inspector, appellant and LPA with proofs of evidence, as the evidence that the third party will give is unlikely to raise new in-depth planning issues. It is also highly unlikely that any inspector will refuse to allow any member of the public who wishes to speak at an inquiry an opportunity to do so (see Procedure at the inquiry, below).

However, if the inquiry in question involves a new airport and local residents are putting forward lengthy and involved evidence about the effect on the residential amenity of flight paths, noise, risk of accidents, etc. and especially if the residents' association are proposing to call or give expert evidence, then they should definitely serve proofs and summaries on the inspector, appellant, LPA and the statutory bodies who will inevitably be involved in a large inquiry of this type.

The rules do not require the appellant, LPA, or statutory bodies to serve copies of their proofs on third parties, although any third party who has notified the DoE of a wish or intention to make a formal appearance will normally find that the appellant and the LPA will furnish copies of their proofs if requested.

If not, the LPA is in any case required by the rules to make proofs, summaries and copies of supporting documents available for public inspection, and where practicable, to allow copies of these documents to be made by any member of the public.

Any third party who wishes to see or obtain copies of all the relevant documents of other parties – from notices of appeal to evidence – should be able to do so.

(vi) Procedure at the inquiry

The rules provide that any person entitled, as of right, to appear at an inquiry may give evidence and may be cross examined by the appellant and LPA. As we have seen, the parties with a legal right to appear are the LPA, appellant, statutory bodies, and in some cases parish councils. An inspector may allow any other third parties to be heard at the inquiry at his or her discretion. That discretion must not be unreasonably withheld, and in practice it means that although non- statutory third parties have no legal right to be heard at an inquiry, in practice virtually anyone who wishes to appear and make representations – from a few sentences to a full third party case – may do so.

For the most part, however, the inspector may conduct the inquiry at his or her discretion, directing in what order the evidence will be heard, and in what order the parties will summarize their cases in 'closing speeches'.

The inspector has power to exclude or refuse to hear evidence or cross examination if he or she regards it as irrelevant or repetitious. The inspector also has power to exclude anyone who is disruptive, to allow any party to amend a case, to take any written representations into account, and to adjourn the inquiry.

Any party at the inquiry has the right to be represented by a barrister, solicitor, planning consultant, other specialist or lay person, or they may represent themselves.

The inspector determines the procedure at an inquiry. In practice, it usually follows this pattern:

- The inspector opens the inquiry, introducing him or herself and indicating whether the inquiry will be determined by him or her or by the Secretary State. He or she outlines a timetable for the day, and if the inquiry is likely to last for a longer period, a provisional outline for the following days. Normally inquiries sit between 10 a.m. and 5 p.m. with an hour for lunch, but the inspector may wish to begin earlier or sit later. The inspector indicates what might be a suitable time to make a formal site visit in the company of the LPA and appellants and deals with any other procedural matters. These include reminding any party who wishes to make an application for costs to do so before the end of the inquiry. The inspector will also ask the parties to draw up a list of conditions which might be appropriate if permission were to be granted.

- Next, the inspector 'takes appearances', normally beginning with the appellant. The appellant or his representative stands, introduces him or herself by name and professional qualification if any, and tells the inspector how many witnesses the appellant will call and what their names are. The inspector then turns to the LPA, who do the same. The inspector will know whether there are any statutory parties appearing, and will turn to them next. Finally if any non-statutory third parties have previously informed the DoE they wish to 'appear' the inspector will take their appearance.

- Finally the inspector will ask whether there is anyone else present who wishes to speak. Anyone who wishes to do so should identify him or herself, and the inspector will make a note of the names of all parties who indicate they wish to say something.

- The inspector will then indicate when the best time will be for such third parties to speak, and normally will ask if they would have difficulty in being present at that time. If there is a problem, no one should feel shy about saying so. Inspectors appreciate that people cannot always be present for the whole of an inquiry, and most will attempt to find a suitable time slot for third parties. It is helpful if third parties have some idea of the way inquiries are likely to proceed, because often members of the public arrive at an inquiry on the first day, anxious to have a say, only to become bored and leave when it turns out they cannot do so immediately.

- The inspector then asks the appellant to begin. The appellant or his or her representative makes an opening speech, outlining the proposal, and why it should be allowed. The appellant's witnesses are then called to read the summaries of their proofs of evidence. As all parties have either been supplied with copies of the full proof of evidence or been able to obtain a copy from the LPA, there is no need to take up inquiry time reading the proof in full. The witness may then be cross examined by the other parties on the full proof.

Normally third party objectors will be allowed to cross examine the appellant's witnesses. If any third parties are attending the inquiry to give evidence in support of the proposal, naturally they will not cross examine the appellant's witness because parties on the same side do not cross examine each other. The same holds true for third party objectors, who do not cross examine the LPA.

- The LPA present their case next, normally without making an opening statement. Their witnesses are called, read their summaries and are cross examined by the appellant (and supporters if appropriate).
- Third parties call their evidence, and may be cross examined. Depending on the case put forward by a third party, evidence may amount to no more than an individual expressing a view. It does not matter in such a case that no formal proof has been prepared, although many individuals wishing to speak at an inquiry will prepare what they want to say in writing beforehand. It takes little more trouble to make copies for the inspector and other parties.

  At the other end of the scale, third parties may wish to present a case raising complex planning issues or matters on which they call expert evidence. In such cases it will have been important to prepare and serve proofs and summaries on the inspector and other parties well in advance.
- Normally after all the evidence of all parties has been heard, the inspector will call on the LPA to make the first closing speech. The LPA will sum up the case it has put forward, emphasizing the strong points and the appellant's weak

points, and highlighting any points in their favour which have come out in the evidence.

- Third parties normally make closing speeches only if they feel this is necessary. A member of the public who has spoken briefly or prepared a short written statement probably will not feel any necessity to make a closing speech. A third party who has presented a substantive case probably will wish to do so.
- The appellant normally makes the final closing speech, getting to 'have the last word'.
- The inspector asks the parties about conditions. In practice the parties will often compare lists of conditions at the lunch adjournment to see how many can be agreed. Third parties may either prepare their own lists of conditions or ask the LPA to put particular ones forward. Failing agreement on conditions by the end of the inquiry, the inspector will hear submissions as to why the conditions which have not been agreed are desirable and/or excessive, appropriate or inappropriate.

If third parties feel particular conditions are appropriate they will be given a chance to explain why.

- Any party with an application for costs must make the application before the close of the inquiry (see Costs, below).
- The inspector announces what arrangements have been made for the formal site visit after the close of the inquiry (if this has not taken place already) and explains what this is for the sake of anyone attending the inquiry who may not know. The inspector will make a formal visit to the appeal site in the company of the appellant and/or the appellant's representative, and in the company of someone from the LPA. The inspector normally announces that if anyone else feels it is useful to be present, they may do so, but all parties are warned against trying to use the occasion to urge their case.

The purpose of the site visit is purely to see the site to enable the inspector to form a view of what effect the proposed development will have. The site visit will usually take place following the close of the inquiry, or if it is dark by then, the inspector will normally make the visit the following morning. The inspector will wish to see the site while all the evidence is fresh in his or her mind.

● The inspector formally announces the inquiry is closed.

(vii) Post-inquiry procedure

If the Secretary of State is determining the appeal, the inspector will make a full report with recommendations to him. The Secretary of State will take the inspector's recommendation as to whether or not to allow the appeal on board, but is not bound to follow it. The Secretary of State will notify all parties to the inquiry and anyone else who has asked to be notified, of the inspector's recommendation and of the Secretary of State's decision and reasons for it.

If the inspector is determining the appeal, copies of his or her decision, findings of fact and reasons for the decision will be sent to all parties and anyone else who has asked to be notified of the decision.

The decision of the inspector or Secretary of State can only be challenged in the High Court.

(viii) Costs

Normally all parties to an inquiry bear their own costs, unlike the position in court where the winning parties costs are borne by the losing party. However, the inspector has power to award costs in some circumstances in the case of a hearing or public planning inquiry. To date there is no power to award costs in an appeal by way of written representations.

There are a number of circumstances justifying an award of costs against an appellant or the LPA, all of them concerned with 'unreasonable' behaviour.

The appellant may be able to recover some or all of his or her costs from the LPA if the LPA:

- failed to comply with the procedures laid down by the rules;
- does not support its objections to the proposal with evidence on planning grounds;
- failed to take government policy and relevant judicial authority into account in maintaining objections to the proposal;
- refused to discuss the planning application with the appellant, refused to provide information requested by the appellant or to ask the appellant for further information relevant to its decision when appropriate;
- refused permission for a modified proposal, following an earlier appeal decision showing a modified form of the proposal refused on the earlier occasion would be acceptable, and there has been no change in circumstances since that decision;
- introduced a new objection or abandoned an existing objection to the proposal at a late stage;
- imposed conditions to a grant of planning permission which are unnecessary, unreasonable, unenforceable, imprecise or irrelevant;
- made unreasonable demands in respect of planning obligations or unreasonably refused to renew an existing or recently expired planning permission;
- unreasonably refused approval for reserve matters on an approved planning permission;
- unreasonably pursued issues in the appeal which were settled when an outline application was approved.

However, an appellant is at risk of having to bear some or all of the LPA's costs if the appellant:

- failed to comply with the procedural requirements in the rules;
- failed to provide a pre-inquiry statement;

- is deliberately uncooperative when requested to provide further information;
- failed to attend the inquiry;
- failed to pursue the appeal;
- introduces new planning issues, a new ground of appeal or new evidence late in the proceedings;
- withdraws from the appeal after being notified by the DoE of the arrangements for the appeal, without good reason or a change of circumstances. However, it is always open to the appellant and the LPA to continue negotiations on the proposal even after an appeal has been lodged, to see if agreement can be reached either by amendment of the application or by agreeing to conditions or planning obligations which would meet the LPA's objections to the scheme and render the appeal unnecessary. This is obviously a change in circumstances justifying withdrawal from the appeal, but the DoE may take the view that had one or both of the parties acted 'reasonably' at an earlier stage the matter could have been resolved before arrangements had been made for the inquiry.
- pursued an appeal which could not reasonably have succeeded – for example if the proposal was in clear contravention of Government planning policy.

If a party to the inquiry introduces new evidence at a late stage, the other parties are entitled to time to consider that evidence and obtain evidence of their own in rebuttal. If a party introduces new evidence at an inquiry, the inspector has power to allow that evidence (and is quite likely to do so because an inspector will be reluctant to bar evidence which may have any bearing on the planning matters at issue) but also has power to award costs of any adjournment necessary to enable the other parties to deal with the new evidence. If the new evidence is of a complex or technical nature, other parties will need enough time to obtain their own expert evidence.

Technically costs may be awarded against third parties but this will only be done in exceptional cases.

The fact that one party has made an application for costs against the other will not affect the outcome of the appeal, as the inspector will consider the issue of costs separately from the planning matters being determined in the appeal.

5

Preparing and Presenting a Case at a Planning Inquiry

The objective of all parties at the inquiry should be (a) to present their own cases as clearly, thoroughly and concisely as possible, and (b) to test the case or cases put forward by opposing parties in an equally thorough, concise and clear fashion. The whole point of a public planning inquiry is to ensure a full public examination of the planning issues before determining the proposal at issue.

It is important for all parties to remember that an inquiry is not an adversarial process, and that there is no need to prove guilt or innocence or that any party is 'right' (although understandably people do often feel strongly about being 'in the right' over planning issues). The inspector may be sympathetic, but his or her job is to determine the planning issues only.

Although planning professionals – barristers, solicitors or planning consultants – are frequently engaged to present parties' cases at the inquiry stage, this is not essential. Most people are quite capable of presenting a good case at a planning inquiry and it is becoming increasingly common to find that in inquiries of any size, non-professionals are becoming quite effective in representing themselves or a group such as a local amenity society or residents' association. No one should feel discouraged from presenting a case at an inquiry because he or she is not a professional.

However, anyone intending to do so should appreciate that the key to presenting a good, and hopefully successful case, is careful and thorough preparation. The more numerous and complex the planning issues, the more effort will be involved, but no one will be penalized for not sounding like a barrister or solicitor or consultant.

The following guidelines should prove useful to appellants and third parties alike, who intend to present cases at public inquiries. In addition, the guidelines should prove helpful to those who instruct professionals to present a case, because a great deal of time and money can be saved by ensuring the instructions given to professionals to present a particular case are clear and to the point.

Any developer or third party who has no previous experience of inquiries may find it helpful to attend all or part of another inquiry to get the 'feel'. Inquiries are open to the public, who may come and go, and it can be quite helpful to see ahead of time that although there is a formality to the proceedings, it is a relaxed formality and not at all intimidating. It is also helpful to see the procedure in practice, because many people do not appreciate that, as objectors or supporters, they will be given an opportunity to speak, but not immediately the inquiry opens. Inquiries are frequently packed with local people who arrive on the first morning, all anxious to make their representations, and who gradually drift away in disappointment when they find they cannot make their representations right away.

Remember that the whole point of a public inquiry is to allow the public to hear and participate in the proceedings, and everyone will be given a chance in due course. If you are a third party wishing to make representations, you should attend on the morning the inquiry opens and indicate to the inspector your wish to speak. The inspector will indicate a rough timetable for the main witnesses to give evidence and indicate when third parties will be invited to give their evidence. The inspector normally asks if any third parties will have difficulty with this timetable. If you really cannot attend at the time indicated, by all means say so, and the inspector will then try to work you in at some other point.

You should remember however, that the inspector cannot write the timetable in stone, because the speed with which the inquiry progresses depends mainly on the length of cross examination of witnesses and any further points the inspector may wish to explore with the witness. It is also possible that unforeseen matters arise which need to be addressed by the main parties in further submissions to the inspector.

If you intend to present a case at an inquiry, you should be aware of the procedural requirements of the relevant rules, (see Procedure at the inquiry, page 43), and consider the following guidelines.

Know your case

While this sounds an obvious point, both developers and third parties sometimes reach the inquiry stage without having thoroughly understood all the practical and policy considerations which may apply in the case of the development proposal at issue. Knowing your case includes knowing what policy considerations apply to the development in question. If the advice given in Chapter 2 was not followed at the application stage, it should be applied now.

This is sound and important advice as a general rule, but there will of course be cases where an objector or supporter only wants to say a few words of at the inquiry objecting to or supporting the appeal proposal. These third parties should not be put off doing so if they feel that looking up development plan policy and government policy is too difficult. Everyone appreciates that as a matter of common sense, if a third party wishes to speak briefly to point out that the appeal proposal will, for example, result in the loss of trees, or overshadow neighbouring properties, etc., there is no need for lengthy submissions citing every relevant policy. In all likelihood these will have been cited anyway by the main parties and repeating them is unnecessary. As long as someone has referred to them, the inspector has the points and will take them into consideration when deciding the appeal.

The following advice, therefore, can be followed by third parties to the extent appropriate to the cases they wish to put at the inquiry.

Advice to appellants

If you are bringing the appeal you will undoubtedly know what your case is (and what are the potential difficulties, if any). At the planning application stage you should have familiarized yourself with the relevant policies in the development plan and any relevant central government advice in the form of circulars or planning policy guidance notes (PPGs) in accordance with the advice in Chapter 2.

For example, if your proposal involves development in a green belt, you will need to know about the policy guidance on development in green belts in PPG 2 'green belts' and DoE Circular 14/84 on green belts.

If your proposal is for development which policy advice suggests would normally not be appropriate, be sure you know why you think your particular scheme ought to be an exception (for example, it would provide a much needed facility).

Be thoroughly prepared as to the planning advantages or benefits which will result if your appeal is allowed: it will create employment/improve an unsightly area/increase the amount of housing/offer local residents a greater choice when shopping, etc., as relevant to your proposal. It is important that you know your own case thoroughly when it comes to preparing your evidence (see Evidence at planning inquiries, page 66).

Knowing your own case also means knowing what the case is against the development, because you will need to discredit these objections as much as possible. In addition to any reasons given by the LPA for refusing permission (or if the appeal is against non-determination, any reasons given indicating on what grounds permission would have been refused had the application been determined), the LPA must make any letters of objection or support for your proposal available to you.

It sometimes happens that, while few letters of objection are written to the LPA at the planning stage, objections have snowballed into a storm of protest by the time the proposal reaches the inquiry stage. As a result, developers have lost inquiries where unforeseen objections and planning issues have been raised by third parties.

LPAs may not always appreciate, or raise, all possible planning objections, but there is nothing to prevent any third party from raising any matter, so long as it is a planning consideration. Particularly with large development proposals, which by their nature are likely to involve large numbers of professional advisers, representatives and witnesses, etc., it is not uncommon for small details to be overlooked, thereby jeopardizing the appellant's case.

One example is the case of large scale development, such as a housing estate, shopping complex or industrial park in a rural area. Leaving aside for the moment the question of any environmental assessment study which may have been prepared (see Chapter 11) in such a case, the issue of the impact on the rural area will undoubtedly be a policy consideration, and the developer will undoubtedly have prepared – at great expense – elaborate plans and possibly a scale model to show that there will be a minimal visual impact from the surrounding roads. At the inquiry the developer often finds that expensively prepared evidence is undermined by indignant local residents turning up at the inquiry to say the development will be not only visible but too prominent a feature in the countryside from public footpaths and rights of way the developer did not know existed, or will affect the setting of listed building of which the developer or his advisers were unaware.

As the developer, 'knowing your case' means more than simply knowing what development you propose to carry out and what policy considerations apply. It also means making every effort to foresee all potential points which might be taken against the development. Remember that third parties have considerable leeway to make representations at an inquiry without prior notice of what these might be. At its most basic level, 'knowing your case' may well involve a thorough investigation of all the features of the surrounding environment. A useful part of the exercise may involve something as simple as walking the surrounding area to try to see the proposal through local residents' eyes.

Advice to third parties

Third parties are also advised to 'know your case'. The very obvious – but often overlooked – first step is to go and look at the plans and any supporting documents so that you know exactly what the development proposal is which will be considered at the inquiry. It can happen that people become extremely antagonistic to development proposals without knowing precisely what is involved. Equally they may be supportive of, or blasé about, a proposal, only to discover to their dismay after the proposal has gone ahead 'We had no idea it would be like that.'

By that time it will be too late to do anything about it.

It is always sensible to check what the plans or documents are which will be relied on at the inquiry, because the appellant may have amended the plans accompanying the original planning application, either to take account of objections, or for a variety of other reasons. These amendments may do away with third party objections or raise new ones, or affect the degree to which the proposal attracts support.

Remember that all the plans and copies of the decision letter refusing permission and all other relevant documents must be made available for public inspection by the LPA, who should also provide facilities for making copies where it is practicable to do so. Most LPAs are extremely helpful to third parties and will try to assist wherever possible. However, it should also be borne in mind that if there is no charge for copying documents, the cost of doing so is passed to local taxpayers.

The larger the development, the more paperwork and plans it is likely to generate. If the appeal proposal involves major development, the plans, and if required, environmental assessment studies, may be very lengthy and difficult to duplicate. If so, it is always worth asking the developer for a copy. The larger and more professional developers will normally respond to a courteous request from third parties for information about proposals going to a public inquiry. It is certainly not in a developer's interest to be obstructive or to be seen to be obstructive to third parties.

If you are one of a group – a local residents association for example – considering making representations at the inquiry, it is probably not necessary to demand a copy of all the documents for every member of your group, either from the LPA or the developer, as one copy could be passed around or copied further by members.

In addition to knowing the developer's case, third parties should also know on what grounds the LPA objects to the proposal, what amendments the LPA might consider would make the proposal acceptable (you may not agree) what development plan policies apply and what DoE circulars and PPGs apply, if any.

If you have done some or all of this research at the planning application stage, there will be less to do now, although, depending on the proposal, you may find that a dauntingly large number of development plan policies apply, as well as several different PPGs and circulars, in whole or in part.

These can be easier to deal with if you have copies, and you can ask the LPA for copies of development plan policies. They may also be able to assist with copies of the government policy documents but strictly speaking they are not obliged to. Otherwise try your local law centre or Citizens Advice Bureau (see Chapter 14).

Once you are thoroughly acquainted with the case the appellant will be making for the proposal at the inquiry, what case the LPA will be making against the proposal and with all the development plan policies and government policies which are relevant, you are in a position to decide what your case is and whether it is worth presenting a full case or whether a letter or brief representation will suffice.

There is no point preparing a long case objecting to the proposal on the same grounds as the LPA. There is no need to duplicate points made by the LPA, although you may feel it useful to make a representation that you or your group support the grounds on which the LPA has objected. You can then give reasons for your support, thus fleshing out and backing up any objections you feel are appropriate.

Local residents are often very effective in backing up development plan policy objections with concrete evidence of their own. For example, the LPA may have refused planning permission on the grounds that the proposal would have an adverse effect on the amenity of neighbouring properties, or that it would be likely to blur the distinction between rural settlements in the green belt, contrary to government policy on development in green belts.

Evidence from local objectors can then explain in more detail what the effects of the proposal are likely to be in their own circumstances.

Likewise, if you support the proposal, there is no need to present a case at great length duplicating the case being made by the developer. It may make far more sense to write a letter in support or to make brief representations in person at the inquiry saying why you support the proposal, and explain what the beneficial effects of the development will be in practice.

There is nothing to prevent either supporters or objectors from indicating that while on the whole they agree permission ought to be granted/refused, they believe that modifications ought to be made or would eliminate objections.

Third parties may find that other third parties will be making the same or similar representations at the inquiry. While all parties will wish to, and indeed are entitled to, have their say, it may make sense to liaise with any parties on the same side. You can often dovetail the evidence of third party cases, or the cases themselves, in a way that mutually supports the points made by all parties on that side, thus reinforcing the total case for or against.

Evidence at the inquiry

At the outset of this section, it is worth reiterating that appellants and third parties intending to make a formal appearance at the inquiry to present a substantial case ought to keep in mind the procedural time limits set out in the relevant inquiry procedure rules for the service of statements of case and proofs of evidence.

Advice to developers

This advice applies to mainly to a developer presenting his or her own case at the inquiry. However, even when professionals are instructed, presenting a case at an inquiry is usually still a team effort, with much depending on the clarity of the developer's instructions as to the conduct of the case. The larger and more complex the issues at the inquiry, the more expert professionals are likely to be employed, but as the developer is bearing the expense, it may save money if the developer is in a position to play a co-ordinating role and know what everyone else on the team is supposed to be doing.

The basic premise that can be made about development – if there is one – is that development ought to go ahead unless there are good planning reasons why it should not. When it comes to preparing evidence for the inquiry, you will start with this premise, but by now it has probably become clear what grounds are being raised by the LPA and objectors as reasons why it should not.

The evidence and witnesses giving it will depend on the nature of the proposal. If the proposal is a minor development scheme, there is no reason you cannot conduct your own case as well as give evidence yourself. However, if you do so you will want to be sure you cite all relevant development plan policies and central government policy, and relate your proposal to them.

Prepare your statement of case to serve on the DoE and LPA. This need only be a short document stating the points you will make in evidence and a list of the plans, documents, development plan policies and central government circulars, PPGs or other documents.

At this stage, if you have not already done so, you should investigate what precedents there are for other similar developments/development of similar sites either permitted by the LPA in the locality, or by an inspector on appeal, as the refusal of permission in your case may be inconsistent with these other cases. If you are going to rely on any other precedents in the area, note them in the list of documents in your statement of case.

Preparing a statement of case is helpful because it is in effect the outline for your proof of evidence.

Proofs of evidence are extremely important and should be prepared – and usually edited – with care. The person giving the evidence begins by identifying him or herself, giving any professional qualifications. The proof then goes on to describe the site of the proposed development, and a description, including a reference to any plans, drawings or other documents if they have been prepared. There should be a section on development plan policy considerations and a section on central government policy advice.

There should be a section emphasizing the planning benefits of the proposal, and a section dealing with any objections. If there are ways these objections could be overcome by conditions or planning obligations you are prepared to accept, specify what they are. However, you will have to judge whether doing so at this stage looks likely to influence the inspector's decision. Finally, if there are precedents for similar proposals or for development on similar sites having been allowed in the areas either by the LPA or an inspector in another appeal, cite them and include the copy of the LPA's decision or the inspector's decision letter in your list of documents.

In citing precedents, the proof should specify how your proposal is similar and why the precedent suggests your development ought to be allowed.

If for some reasons the precedents may not be entirely applicable to your case (and few sites and development proposals are exactly identical) acknowledge any weaknesses (before they are dragged out of you in cross examination by the LPA) in the precedents. You can then emphasize the similarities much more effectively.

Many proofs of evidence could benefit from editing, as too often they are repetitious with a tendency to ramble. Any developer drafting his own proof – or preparing a proof with the help of advisers is advised to go over it several times, and where possible 'tighten it up'. Obviously it is essential to include all relevant information in the proof – after all it is the full statement of the developer's case – but once a point is made there is no need to repeat it over and over. Aim to make proofs thorough, concise and to the point.

Remember that any proof over 1500 words must be summarized to that length. The witness giving the evidence will read the summary at the inquiry, but the inspector and all other parties will have copies of the full proof, and it is the full proof on which the witness is then cross examined by other parties.

Insofar as possible, when preparing proofs try to anticipate the points on which you will be cross examined by other parties, and deal with them in the proof.

Any plans or drawings or other documents you are relying on will be part of your evidence. Be sure they are accurate, because inspectors are extremely precise about site plans and detailed drawings. Any plans, drawings or representations of how the finished development will look will be subject to cross examination and any technical errors or misrepresentations exposed as a result are likely to prove very irritating to the inspector.

Advice to third parties

Third parties have considerable leeway about the form and content of their evidence, and what this is will depend very much on the circumstances and the particular development proposal before the inquiry.

As already noted (see Procedure at the Inquiry, pp 49–50), after the inspector takes appearances he or she will ask whether anyone else is present who wishes to speak. Anyone may respond that they do wish to do so and they will not be prevented from speaking because no formal proof has been submitted. In fact it is rare that anyone wishing to speak briefly prepares anything like a formal proof, although it can be helpful – although not necessary – to write the points you wish to make in a letter or brief statement which can be copied to the inspector, the appellant and the LPA.

Such a brief written statement need not refer to development plan policy or central Government policy considerations, and the only important thing to remember is to try and put your points across in 'planning terms'. If the proposal will affect you and your property, try to couch what you say in terms of 'the effects of the proposal on the residential amenity of the neighbourhood' or words to that effect. You can then go on to say 'for example in my case the effects will be...'.

If you make representations as a third party, the appellant will be given an opportunity to cross examine you if you are an objector, and the LPA may wish to cross examine you if you are a supporter.

Organizing the point or points you wish to make in a simple written statement – hand-written is perfectly acceptable – is useful in two ways. It concentrates your mind on the points to be made, and it is helpful for the inspector to have the points in writing to take away from the inquiry. The inspector will consider your evidence, together with all the other documents in the inquiry, when deciding whether to allow the appeal.

Increasingly third parties such as local amenity groups or residents' associations wish to put in a more comprehensive written statement, sometimes referring to policy considerations. This is normally acceptable to the inspector who will permit these statements to be read. Again, the appellant and the LPA will be given the opportunity to cross examine objectors or supporter, as applicable.

Third parties may also call expert evidence if they wish. If so, the DoE, the appellant and the LPA should have advance notice, because they must be given an opportunity to have their own experts consider the evidence, and if appropriate, call evidence in rebuttal.

Third parties may of course instruct professionals to present their case. Any party instructing a professional representative should appreciate that representatives can only be as good as the instructions they receive.

Presenting evidence at the inquiry

Witnesses usually sit at a table, so proofs and plans can be spread out and referred to. If you are giving evidence at an inquiry for the first time, it may help to go along to another inquiry first to see what to expect.

Witnesses are invited by the inspector to read their proofs, or summaries if the proofs are long, and they may then be cross examined by other parties. They may also be asked questions by the inspector on any points on which the inspector feels further clarification is helpful. Normally the main parties' witnesses, especially expert witnesses, can expect a grilling in cross examination by the other main party or parties. Any third party waiting a turn to speak may understandably be filled with alarm.

If so, it may be reassuring to know that in practice, cross examination of third parties is normally much gentler. Expert witnesses and LPA officers are used to fierce cross examinations, but the inspector will not be impressed if it appears that a member of the public who wishes to speak is being harassed by another party in cross examination.

However, third parties should think through carefully what they wish to say, and be prepared for questions on their evidence. It is always advisable to have written the evidence down, even in a simple letter form, with numbered points, and copies made for the inspector, the appellant, the LPA and a few spare copies for other third parties, if any. If you are reading your evidence and you think of something you wish to add, by all means do so. The inspector will make a note of it.

Cross examination

All parties who intend making formal appearances – including third parties putting forward a substantial case – will have exchanged proofs of evidence in advance. This will allow everyone a chance to go through the evidence of other parties very carefully and identify the points on which it differs from the evidence any other party is giving.

The point of cross examination is to ask questions of the other side to lead them to agree with your conclusions about the proposal. Questions for cross examination need to be carefully prepared to lead the party being cross examined gradually to the conclusion the cross examining party seeks.

Make the questions short, and if the witness being cross examined goes off on a tangent (an old trick to throw everyone off the scent of the original question) point out that he or she has gone off on a tangent and ask the question again. It is up to the party asking the questions not to let the witness evade having to give an answer.

Avoid putting questions that are really statements of your own views. The witness is not going to agree with you and putting questions in this way will not lead him or her to disagree with the evidence he or she has just given. Stick to questions of fact as much as possible.

If you are challenging a witness's opinion, or the conclusions drawn from the facts in evidence, deal with the facts first, to demonstrate that the witness's opinion, or conclusion on those facts, is questionable.

Closing speeches

In the majority of inquiries only the appellant and the LPA make closing speeches. However, if third parties are putting a substantial case, they may indicate to the inspector that they wish to do so. Remember that it is unnecessary to repeat at length any points or submissions made by the main parties. A third party case which expands on points already made by other parties may deal with those points by 'adopting' points before dealing with the other issues of the third party case.

Closing speeches are important in that they draw together the evidence in the case in a way that supports the case of the party making the speech. It is often said that it is difficult to know what an inquiry is really about until the closing speech stage, when the parties will be trying to address what have, by this time, emerged as the salient issues.

In reaching a decision, the inspector will have to identify the main planning issues of the appeal. Anyone making a closing speech should indicate what that party believes them to be, why these are the issues, and how the evidence supports the party's case on these issues. Any party making a closing speech will probably refer to the relevant development plan policies, and government policy advice. Frequently government policy advice indicates the way in which development plan policy ought to be viewed or applied in determining appeals such as the present one.

Again, it may be helpful to attend another inquiry to get the feel of the way in which the parties sum up their own cases and rebut opposing cases in closing speeches.

Planning inquiry checklist

- Check the relevant procedural rules for timetable as to:
  - Serving of statement of case
  - Serving of proofs of evidence
- Prepare proofs of evidence
  - Serve on other parties according to the timetable in rules
  - Prepare and serve a summary of each proof over 1500 words
- Third parties may write letters of representation to either or

both the LPA and the DoE instead of making formal appearance.

- Any third party wishing to speak briefly at the inquiry will not be prevented from doing so even if they have not written to the DoE indicating what representations will be made. In such circumstances it is not necessary to serve statements of case and proofs unless required by the DoE.
- Any third party intending to put forward a substantive case should inform the DoE who may then require a statement of case. If so proofs of evidence, and summaries if appropriate, should be served on the DoE and other parties.
- Ensure there are at least three copies of all proofs, summaries, plans, drawings and photographs.

Appeals by written representations

Procedure

The procedure for appeals by written representations is simpler and, for obvious reasons, less formal than that for appeals heard in an open public inquiry. Appeals by written representation are governed by the Town and Country Planning (Appeals) (Written Representations Procedure) Regulations 1987.

It should be noted that the only parties who can determine whether an appeal is heard by written representations are the appellant and the LPA. Third parties have no rights as to how an appeal is heard, but parties who make representations to the LPA in respect of the planning application subject of the appeal will be notified if an inquiry by written representations is to be held, in order that third parties affected by the proposal may have an opportunity to make their own representations in writing just as they would have if the inquiry were held in public.

Upon receiving the notice of appeal from the appellant, the Secretary of State will notify all parties, including third parties who have previously made representations in respect of the proposal, of the time within which written representations must be made to him and the place where they should be sent.

Preparing and presenting a case by way of written representation

The same principles apply as in presenting a case before a public inquiry. It is important for all parties to identify the planning issues involved and to know what development plan policies apply in order that the case for or against, or seeking modifications, fits into the development plan.

There is no need to make long-winded representations – the Secretary of State will not be impressed by sheer length. However, it is important to make all the points you believe are relevant, and to give some thought to the case that other parties are making in order to say why you believe they are right or wrong. Parties making representations may submit relevant supporting documentation.

Unlike public inquiries, there will be no cross examination of the evidence before the Secretary of State.

In general, the advice given in this chapter about preparing and presenting a case at a planning inquiry also applies to preparing and presenting a case by written representation.

Barristers open their planning briefs

6

Stage (3) of the Planning System: Appeals to the High Court Against an Inspector's Decision

Section 288 of the Town and Country Planning Act provides that anyone who is 'aggrieved' by an inspector's decision may challenge the validity of that decision in the High Court. The proceedings under this section are similar to, but obviously not the same as, judicial review. The definition of persons who may be 'aggrieved' is wide. Aside from the LPA and appellant, it has been interpreted broadly by the courts as nearly anyone who might be aggrieved by the decision, including third parties, and in some cases, even parties who were not third parties at the inquiry, such as subsequent purchasers of land affected by the inspector's decision.

Grounds of appeal

Such an appeal against or, properly speaking, challenge to, the validity of an inspector's decision can only be brought on limited grounds. These are that the inspector 's decision was

(1) not within the powers of the Act or (2) that any relevant requirements were not complied with.

What do these grounds mean?

(i) Not within the powers of the Act

This depends on whether the inspector's decision letter reveals an 'error of law'. We have seen above that the duty of the inspector, as laid down by the Act, is effectively to step into the shoes of the LPA in determining the appeal. The inspector comes afresh to the planning application, and deals with it as if the application had been made to him or her, i.e. the Secretary of State in the first place.

The inspector must perform the same exercise as the LPA performs when determining an application. This exercise requires that each application be determined on its merits, having regard to the provisions of the development plan and all material considerations. If the application/appeal is determined in any other way, this is an error of law, and the decision will not have been reached in accordance with the requirements of the Act.

Arguably an inspector's decision letter would disclose an error of law if it was not clear from the letter whether a development plan policy relevant to the development in question was taken into account in reaching the decision. However, everything depends on the wording of the letter, which may be open to more than one interpretation.

(ii) Relevant requirements not complied with

This means procedural requirements have not been complied with. However, anyone intending to challenge the validity of a decision on this basis will need to be able to show that they were prejudiced in some way by the failure to comply with procedural requirements.

The procedural requirements which must be followed are those laid down by the relevant rules. However, a party may also be prejudiced if there is a failure to observe something called the rules of natural justice. Natural justice requires that everyone is entitled to a hearing, and that no one should be judge in his own case. A failure to observe the principles of natural justice could be regarded both as a failure to have regard to all material considerations (thus resulting in a decision outside the powers of the Act, which requires regard to be had to all material considerations) as well as a breach of a procedural requirement.

What can be challenged in the inspector's decision

Inspectors send a copy of their decision letter to all parties who put in a formal appearance at an inquiry, and almost always ask any last minute third parties who indicate they wish to speak whether they wish to be informed of the decision. The inspector will make a note of the names and addresses of those parties who wish to receive a copy of the decision. The inspector's decision letter will set out the findings of fact the inspector has made on the evidence at the inquiry, will identify the relevant planning issues, and will give reasons for determining those issues to produce the decision reached. The reasons should be clear and comprehensible.

What cannot be challenged is the inspector's findings of fact, as the courts take the view that the inspector who heard the evidence first hand and saw the site must be in the optimum position to make findings of fact. The courts will not therefore, second guess the inspector as to what finding of fact ought to have been made. As the inspector's findings of fact will be written in stone if any appeal is contemplated, this underlines the importance of presenting clear, compelling and well-prepared evidence on the facts at the inquiry.

Anyone who believes the inspector's decision is wrong and that they are 'aggrieved' as a result should appreciate that even if there are grounds for a challenge to the validity of the decision in the High Court, at the end of the day, there is always the risk of losing the case and having to pay the other side's costs.

In some cases third party objectors who feel the inspector's decision was flawed can persuade the LPA – obviously also opposed to the proposal – to challenge the decision. Particularly in cases where the planning issues involved have affected a large number of people and/or attracted publicity, third parties can sometimes pressure the LPA to consider the possibilities for an appeal to the High Court. Equally, LPAs who are concerned about the precedent which may be set if a particular type of proposal is allowed may be concerned to mount a challenge to the validity of the decision if at all possible.

The case is arguably more difficult for the appellant who is refused permission, who does not have the option of seeking to persuade the LPA to appeal on his behalf. An appellant who is refused permission should not make a similar application within two years of the decision unless there has been a change of circumstances, but given the length of time for cases to be scheduled for a High Court hearing date, it will often make sense to wait out the two-year period and re-apply for permission. If so, the developer may wish to consider whether any elements of the proposal ought to be amended to avoid objections previously raised being successfully sustained on a second occasion.

Any challenge to the validity of an inspector's decision must be made within six weeks of the decision letter's being signed and date stamped by the inspector, not six weeks from receipt of the letter. Compliance with the time limit means that the notice of motion must be filed in the Crown Office within the six-week period. The time limit is strictly applied.

Advice to any party contemplating an appeal against an inspector's decision is twofold: first, read the decision letter very carefully. Second, in view of the risk of having to pay the other side's costs if an appeal is lost, it is probably advisable to take specialist legal advice as to the strength of the case and the ultimate prospects of success.

7

Breaches of Planning Control – Enforcement Action

Any development or change of use which requires planning permission is unauthorized and unlawful if it is carried out without that permission. It is also unlawful to implement a conditional planning permission without complying with the conditions attached.

The LPA has broad powers to investigate and take steps to cause the unauthorized development to be removed and the land restored to its previous condition, to require the unauthorized use to cease, or to enforce compliance with conditions attached to a planning permission. They may serve enforcement notices, or take more drastic and immediate action by the serving of stop notices or by obtaining an injunction.

It is helpful at this stage to return briefly to the planning system cake, with its elements of law, government policy and public consultation, because all three elements play a role in the exercise of planning control through enforcement proceedings.

Determining whether there has been a breach of planning control

In some cases the LPA only becomes aware that there has been a breach of planning control through complaints made by local residents. Anyone who is concerned that some development or activity may be in breach of planning controls should contact the enforcement officer at the LPA, preferably in writing, with a copy to local councillors. It always helps if the local councillors are informed of their constituents' concerns on planning (or indeed any) matters. As with everything else, the greater the number of complaints, and the more people to whom they are made, the more likely it is that action will be taken.

If the LPA believes there has been a breach of planning control, the enforcement officer may go on to the land to investigate, and will report back to the planning committee.

Planning contravention notice

In the first instance the LPA may decide to serve a planning contravention notice, requiring the owner or occupier of the land to provide further information as to any operations or activities on the land or in relation to any conditions which may have been attached to planning permission granted for development on the land. The owner or occupier on whom the planning contravention notice is served must provide the information requested, in writing. In addition, the notice may provide that the person on whom it is served may either apply for planning permission or give a voluntary undertaking to cease the activity complained of.

The planning contravention notice will also inform the person on whom it is served that a failure to respond will in all probability result in enforcement proceedings being taken.

In some cases, the owner or occupier of land may not have appreciated that building, development, use or other operations on land were potentially in breach of planning control. However, a planning contravention notice should never be ignored.

It is a criminal offence punishable by a fine to fail to comply with a planning contravention notice within 21 days or to recklessly or knowingly provide false information.

Use of discretion by LPA

The LPA will not in every case enforce against unauthorized development, change of use or failure to carry out development in accordance with any conditions attached to a grant of planning permission.

Even if their investigations reveal that a breach of planning control has occurred, the LPA is not required by law to enforce against *every* breach of planning control, but may exercise its discretion as to whether or not it is 'expedient' to do so, having regard to the provisions of the development plan and all other material considerations. However, when exercising that discretion, the LPA will have in mind the possibility that there is a right of appeal against a decision to take enforcement proceedings. This appeal takes the form of a public inquiry, at which the LPA may have to justify the reasonableness of its decision.

If the LPA feels that it may be a difficult decision to justify at a later stage, it will be less likely to proceed. It is obviously much easier to justify a decision to proceed if there is evidence of complaints from local residents.

While the Town and Country Planning Act provides for the enforcement powers of LPAs as a tool of planning control, government policy lays down guidelines for the approach LPAs should take when deciding whether and how to exercise these powers.

Government policy indicates LPAs should apply the following guiding principles:

(i)   consider whether enforcement action is in the public interest
(ii)   consider whether a failure to take necessary enforcement action, or effective enforcement action, might amount to maladministration
(iii)   consider whether the enforcement action taken is appropriate to the severity of the breach of control or its effects
(iv)   where the LPA has attempted unsuccessfully to negotiate with the owner or occupier of the land to remedy the negative effects of the breach, these negotiations should not prevent necessary enforcement action being taken.

Immunity from enforcement proceedings – time limits

Some breaches of planning control, while unlawful, are nevertheless immune from enforcement action. In the case of unauthorized development which consists of building, mining,

Barchester City Council
Town and Country Planning Act 1971
(as amended)
Enforcement Notice

Whereas:
(1) It appears to the Barchester City Council ('the Council'), being the local
planning authority for the purposes of section 87 of the Town and Country Planning Act 1971 ('the Act') in this matter, that there has been
a breach of planning control within the period of four years before
the date of issue of this notice on the land or premises ('the land')
described in Schedule 1 below.
(2) The breach of planning control which appears to have taken place
consists in the carrying out of building, engineering, mining
or other operations described in Schedule 2, without the grant
of planning permission required for that development.
(3) The Council consider it expedient, having regard to the
provisions of the development plan and to all other material
considerations, to issue this enforcement notice, in exercise
of their powers contained in the said section 87, for the
reasons set out in the annex to this notice

NOTICE IS HEREBY GIVEN that the Council require that the steps specified in Schedule 3 below be taken in order to remedy the breach within
the period specified in respect of each step in that Schedule.

THIS NOTICE WILL TAKE EFFECT, subject to the provisions of section
88(10) of the Act, on 1st April 1988

Issued 14 February 1988
City Hall
Barchester

Signed
OBADIAH SLOPE
Chief Executive
and City Solicitor

SCHEDULE 1
Land or premises to which this notice relates
The Old Hospital, The Close, Barchester; shown edged red on the
attached plan.
SCHEDULE 2
Alleged breach of planning control
Construction of new pedestrian access to the Close, and erection of
single-storey extension at east side of main building.
SCHEDULE 3
Steps required to be taken
(i)   Blocking-up of new access, in materials and style exactly
       matching those of the existing wall: to be completed by 15
       May 1988.
(ii)   Demolition of new single-storey extension, and making good
       wall of original building: to be completed by 15 May 1988.
(iii) Landscaping of garden to its former state: to be completed
       by 1 September 1988.

Figure 4 Enforcement notice

engineering or other operational development on, over or under land, no enforcement action may be taken after four years have elapsed from the unauthorized development having been substantially completed.

If there has been an unauthorized change of use of any building to use as a single dwelling house, enforcement action must be taken within four years of the date on which the change of use began.

In the case of any other unauthorized development or change of use, enforcement action must be taken within ten years of the date of the breach of planning control.

However, if the LPA has acted within the time limits to enforce against a breach of planning control, they may take further enforcement action within four years of the earlier enforcement action, notwithstanding the fact the time limits have expired.

If the LPA does not take enforcement action within the appropriate time limits, its right to do so lapses and the uses and operations become lawful and no longer a breach of planning control.

Enforcement notices

If the LPA decides it is expedient to take enforcement action, having regard to the development plan and all material considerations – including government policy advice – it will normally issue an enforcement notice. A copy of the notice must be served within 28 days of issue to the occupier of the land to which the notice refers, or any other party having an interest which might be materially affected by the notice.

Service of enforcement notices

The notice may be served in a number of ways: by post, by hand or by personal service. If the names of the owner and/or occupier are unknown, the notice may simply be addressed to 'the owner' or 'the occupiers' and served at the site. If the site is unoccupied when the notice is served, the enforcement officer may serve it effectively by affixing the notice in some conspicuous place on the site.

Contents of the enforcement notice

Enforcement notices must specify the following:

- the land to which the notice applies
- what is the breach of planning control subject of the notice
- whether this is development without planning permission or a failure to comply with a condition or limitation of a planning permission
- what steps must be taken to remedy the breach of planning control
- what planning purpose each step is intended to achieve or what harm is to be remedied
- the date on which the notice takes effect, or comes into force, and the period allowed for compliance with the notice
- the LPA's reasons for serving the notice.

The notice must also be accompanied by an explanatory note or information informing the recipient of the right to appeal against the notice, and if the right is exercised, the requirement that the grounds of appeal must be specified.

Anyone receiving an enforcement notice has several options: comply with the notice, appeal against the notice to the Secretary of State, or negotiate with the LPA to see if agreement can be reached to deal with the breach of planning control in some other way. If such an arrangement can be negotiated to meet the concerns of the LPA over the breach of planning control, the LPA has discretion to withdraw or amend the notice. The LPA now has power to withdraw a notice even after it has come into effect. The LPA may also relax or waive any requirements of the notice.

Ignoring the enforcement notice is not an option. Anyone who fails to comply with an enforcement notice by the date specified for compliance commits a criminal offence, punishable by a fine of up to £20,000 by magistrates and if convicted by the crown court, by a fine at the court's discretion.

Appeals against enforcement notices

The party on whom the enforcement notice was served may appeal to the Secretary of State, as may any other person with an interest in the land. Anyone wishing to appeal must do so before the time specified on the notice as to when the notice takes effect. Once it takes effect, there is no right of appeal. Time limits are strictly enforced.

Section 174 of the 1990 Town and Country Planning Act specifies seven grounds of appeal. These are:

1   that planning permission for the breach complained of ought to be granted (this ground applies automatically as a deemed application for planning permission, although it should always be specified by the appellant);
2   that the matters specified as amounting to a breach of planning control have not occurred;
3   even if the matters specified as amounting to a breach of planning control have occurred, they do not amount to a breach of planning control;
4   that at the date the notice was issued, no enforcement action could be taken against the matters alleged as the breach;
5   the enforcement notice was not properly served;
6   that the steps the notice requires to be taken to remedy the breach of control are excessive;
7   that the time allowed for compliance is too short.

These grounds are listed on the notice of appeal form the appellant must complete. Anyone contemplating an appeal may find a useful source of advice in the Department of the Environment's booklet, *Enforcement Notice Appeals*. Copies are obtainable from:

Department of the Environment
Tollgate House
Houlton Street
Bristol BS2 9DJ

A fee is payable upon appealing against an enforcement notice because it is simultaneously deemed to be an application for planning permission. The fee is the same as would be applicable if permission were being applied for.

As with appeals against refusal of planning permission, the LPA will advertise notices of the enforcement appeal, and will often notify anyone living in the vicinity of the appeal site if it appears such local residents will be affected by the outcome of the appeal.

Enforcement notice appeals

The procedures for an enforcement notice appeal are similar to the rules governing planning inquiry procedure, and are the 1981 Town and Country Planning (Enforcement) (Inquiries Procedure) Rules. The inquiry can be dealt with by way of written representations or by way of a public inquiry before an inspector at the request of either the appellant or the LPA.

It must be emphasized that it is essential for the appellant to specify the grounds of appeal. Because the time for the appeal to be lodged may be short, it is acceptable for the appellant to specify generally which grounds will be relied upon on the appeal form when submitting it to the DoE. However, this must be followed by a full written statement of the grounds of appeal and a brief summary of the facts on which the appellant will rely.

The LPA will be required to prepare and serve a statement on the Secretary of State and the appellant. This statement will specify the LPA's response to each ground of appeal raised by the appellant, and whether they are prepared to grant planning permission for the deemed planning application.

Third parties who wish to make representations in writing may do so to the DoE and/or the LPA, in the same way as they would do in respect of an application for planning permission.

As in planning inquiries, the LPA must make all pre-inquiry statements and documents available for public inspection, and allow interested parties to take copies if it is practicable.

The Planning Inspectorate

An Executive Agency in the Department of the Environment and the Welsh Office

Town and Country Planning Act 1990 (as amended)

For DOE use only

Enforcement notice appeal to the Secretary of State for the Environment

Ref. no. APP/..................................

- IMPORTANT: Do not delay. Your completed Appeal form must be received (or posted in time to be received) in the Department before the date on which the Council have stated that the Enforcement Notice shall take effect (see section 8 for more details). You are strongly advised to send the completed form well before this date.
- Before you complete this form, please read the explanatory booklet "Enforcement Notice Appeals – A Guide to Procedure". If you do not have a copy, the Council can provide one.

1. Appellant's details *(Please use BLOCK LETTERS)*

Full name and address...

.... Postcode ....

Telephone number.. Reference number ....

Name and address of any agent or professional representative to whom letters should be sent ....

....

.... Postcode ....

Telephone number.. Reference number ....

2. Appeal and grounds *(Please use a separate form for each enforcement notice)*

I appeal, (on the appellant's behalf)* under section 174 of the Town and Country Planning Act 1990 (as amended), against the enforcement notice dated.................................. issued by ....
Council relating to land at ....
....

I appeal on the ground(s) in section 174(2) of the 1990 Act, indicated by a cross (X) in the appropriate box below:

☐ **Ground (a)** that, in respect of any breach of planning control which may be constituted by the matters stated in the notice, planning permission ought to be granted or, as the case may be, the condition or limitation concerned ought to be discharged;

☐ **Ground (b)** that those matters have not occurred;†

☐ **Ground (c)** that those matters (if they occurred) do not constitute a breach of planning control;

☐ **Ground (d)** that, at the date when the notice was issued, no enforcement action could be taken in respect of any breach of planning control which may be constituted by those matters;

☐ **Ground (e)** that copies of the enforcement notice were not served as required by section 172;

☐ **Ground (f)** that the steps required by the notice to be taken, or the activities required by the notice to cease, exceed what is necessary to remedy any breach of planning control which may be constituted by those matters or, as the case may be, to remedy any injury to amenity which has been caused by any such breach;

☐ **Ground (g)** that any period specified in the notice in accordance with section 173(9) falls short of what should reasonably be allowed.

† Please note that the only purpose of an appeal on **Ground (b)** is to maintain that the Council's allegation in the enforcement notice has not occurred, **as a matter of fact.**

* *delete as appropriate*

DOE 14069 (Revised 10/94) 1 FED 0448 10/94 DDP

Figure 5 **Notice of appeal against enforcement notice**

3. Appeal site

Full address of the appeal site and, if possible, the National Grid Reference *(refer to an Ordnance Survey map for help)*

....

.... Postcode (if any) ....

Please state your legal interest in the appeal site: *owner/occupier/tenant/lessee/licensee/other *(please specify below)*

....

* *delete as appropriate*

4. Other appeals

Have you made any other appeals to the Secretary of State involving this or any related land?　　Yes ☐　No ☐
(Please indicate by a cross (X) in the appropriate box)

If Yes, please provide details:

Type of appeal	Date of appeal	DOE reference no. *(if known)*

5. Written representations

Do you agree to have your appeal dealt with on the basis of written statements by the parties　　Yes ☐　No ☐
and an inspection of the site by an officer of the Department?
(Please indicate by a cross (X) in the appropriate box)

If Yes, can the whole site, including the alleged breach of planning control, be seen clearly　　Yes ☐　No ☐
from the road or other public land?
*(Please indicate by a cross (X) in the appropriate box, to help the Department decide whether
the officer will need to enter the site and therefore have to be accompanied on the site visit)*

Please note: Although you may agree to the appeal being dealt with by written representations, the Secretary of State
may find it essential to hold a Public Local Inquiry.

6. Statement of facts

*Failure to provide facts may result in the dismissal of the appeal or the
refusal to consider a ground of appeal without supporting facts.*

Please state here the facts in support of **each** one of the seven grounds of appeal (a) to (g) you have marked with an "X"
in section 2 of this form.

Please continue on the next page

2

Figure 5 **Notice of appeal against enforcement notice**
(Continued)

6. Statement of facts *(continued)*

Please turn over

3

Figure 5 Notice of appeal against enforcement notice
(Continued)

7. Signature

I attach a copy of the relevant enforcement notice to this form.
I confirm that this appeal form contains an appeal/appeals* against only one enforcement notice and that I have sent a copy of this form to the Council with any supporting documents.

Signature.. Date ....

* *delete as appropriate*

8. Checking and sending the appeal

Before you send this appeal to the Department. please check that you have:

● completed the whole form, including the statement of facts (section 6);

● enclosed a copy of the enforcement notice.

Now send one copy of this appeal by **first class post** to:

The Planning Inspectorate (PINS AA 4), PO Box 326, Bristol BS99 7XF

The appeal must arrive (or be posted in time to arrive in the normal course of post) in the Department not later than the day before the date, stated by the Council, for the enforcement notice to take effect.
If the notice takes effect on a Saturday, this will be the preceding Friday or the preceding Thursday if the Friday is a Public Holiday. If the notice takes effect on a Sunday, Monday or Public Holiday, this will be the last working day before the Holiday or the last day on which post is delivered before the Sunday or Holiday.

If you wish to have proof that your appeal has been received by the Department, you should send it by Post Office "recorded delivery" for which an extra charge is payable. **As this service normally takes longer than standard post, please allow extra time if you use it.**

To save time, you may fax this appeal form and the Council's enforcement notice to the Department's office in Bristol, on 0117 987 8782 or, if unobtainable, 0117 987 8679. You may also deliver, by hand, to any Department of the Environment office; if you do so, please ensure that the receiving officer gives you or your courier a receipt showing the date and time of delivery.

Please note that a fee is normally payable for the deemed application for planning permission arising on an enforcement appeal *(as explained in the booklet "Enforcement Notice Appeals · A Guide to Procedure")*. No money should be enclosed with this appeal form. We will notify you of the fee payable when your appeal has been accepted.

Please send a second copy of the appeal form, and any supporting documents to the Council who issued the enforcement notice.

4

Figure 5 **Notice of appeal against enforcement notice**
(Continued)

Dual nature of enforcement notice appeals

Enforcement notice appeals have a dual role, one to deal with grounds of appeal (2) through (7) and one to consider the deemed application for planning permission on ground (1).

Grounds of appeal (2) – (7)

The onus is on the appellant to establish the case on such of these grounds as are relied upon on the balance of probabilities.

As part of the case being made on any of these grounds, the appellant will probably wish to challenge the LPA's decision that it was 'expedient' to take enforcement action, having regard to the development plan and all material considerations, including central government policy guidelines as to the exercise of the LPA's discretion in taking enforcement action.

The deemed planning application under ground (1)

The test here is the same as that which applies in relation to all applications for planning permission: the application must be considered on its merits, having regard to the development plan and all material considerations.

Obviously some, if not most, of the evidence of both the appellant and the LPA will be the same for both aspects of the inquiry. However, the appellant, and any third parties, should not lose sight of the distinction between the two aspects of the appeal and ensure that both are adequately addressed in the inquiry, both in the evidence and in submissions on the two aspects. Cross examination of the other parties will also need to be anticipated and prepared accordingly.

Third parties' right to be heard

There is often a substantial amount of third party interest in enforcement notice appeals, because in many cases local residents have complained to the LPA about the breach of planning control which caused the enforcement notice to be served in the first place.

Equally, there may be a show of local support for the owner or occupier of the land and the activities which are the subject of the notice.

The Enforcement Notice Inquiry Rules provide for a greater list of parties who may appear at the inquiry as of right. Technically speaking, other third parties are in the same position as in planning inquiries. Therefore, although there is no absolute requirement to do so, any third party who wishes to make substantial representations or make a formal appearance at an enforcement notice appeal should notify the DoE. The Secretary of State will notify that party whether a pre-inquiry statement needs to be served.

In particular, the rules provide that if two or more people have a similar interest in the subject of the inquiry, the inspector may ask one person to speak for that group.

Procedure at enforcement notice appeals

Enforcement notice appeal procedure is almost exactly the same as in planning inquiries (see Chapter 4). As regards any third parties who have not written to the DoE indicating they wish to object to or support the activities complained of in the notice, it is normally the case that the inspector will ask, after taking formal appearances, whether anyone else wishes to speak. As at planning inquiries, such third parties speak at the inspector's discretion, but it is almost unknown for an inspector to refuse anyone a right to be heard at a convenient moment.

As at planning inquiries, third parties should appreciate that, although they will undoubtedly be allowed to speak, they should not be discouraged because they are not allowed to speak right away.

No third party should feel discouraged from making simple representations because other parties are making substantial cases with long proofs of evidence. Public inquiries are intended as a forum for the public to have a say. Often brief representations from third parties can be extremely helpful to an inspector in drawing some aspect of the matter under consideration to his or her attention. In some cases it is only third parties who may have

noticed some relevant point which has been overlooked by everyone else.

In planning inquiries, parties give evidence about the likely impact of development or change of use not yet carried out. In an appeal against an enforcement notice, evidence can be given of the actual impact of the use or development on the local environment, because that use or development has already been or is being carried out.

(i) Evidence at enforcement notice appeals

The preparation of evidence by both the appellant and third parties should be prepared as in planning inquiries. Aside from third parties wishing to make fairly simple representations, anyone presenting a case should be aware of the relevant development plan policies, government policy, and anything else which might amount to a 'material consideration' in the circumstances, including precedents of other inspectors' decisions in similar enforcement appeals.

However, the focus of that evidence needs to be shifted slightly so that both aspects of the enforcement notice appeal are seen to be thoroughly addressed. Although the evidence on both aspects of the appeal will be the same, it is a good idea to make it quite clear how the evidence applies to the deemed application for planning permission and to the grounds of appeal (2) – (7).

As well as addressing grounds (2) – (7) the appellant will undoubtedly also address whether the LPA have followed government policy advice in deciding if it was 'expedient' to take enforcement action.

If third parties feel strongly that enforcement action should have been taken, it does not hurt to support the LPA by saying so to the inspector.

(ii) Site visit

As with an application for planning permission, the inspector will make a site visit at some convenient point in the inquiry or at the end of the inquiry. No one should attempt to make further representations, as the inspector cannot take them into account and will probably be extremely irritated by any party's attempt to use the site visit to further a particular case. The site visit is for inspection purposes only.

(iii) Notification of the result of the appeal

As with an the decision following a planning appeal, the inspector determining an enforcement notice appeal will notify the main parties and any third parties who request to be informed of the decision.

The Secretary of State/inspector has wide powers to quash the notice altogether, to correct it, to vary it or to grant planning permission for some or all of the development which is the subject of the deemed planning application. If the enforcement notice concerns non-compliance with a condition attached to planning permission, the Secretary of State/inspector may discharge the condition.

The enforcement notice is of no effect until the inspector decides whether or not it should be upheld.

(iv) Withdrawal of an appeal

The appellant may withdraw the appeal at any stage. The effect is to bring the enforcement notice into operation from that time.

(v) Costs

Costs may be awarded by the Secretary of State even if the appeal has been withdrawn. If an application for costs is made at the inquiry, the inspector will report to the Secretary of State any relevant considerations on the application and may make recommendations. The position on costs is similar to the basis on which they are awarded in planning inquiries, on the grounds of unreasonable behaviour.

Appeals to the High Court against the enforcement appeal decision

The parties who may appeal to the High Court against an inspector's decision on an enforcement appeal are limited to the appellant, the

LPA and to any person having an interest in the land to which the enforcement notice applies.

Unlike the case with appeals against a planning inspector's decision, any party wishing to appeal the determination of an enforcement notice appeal must first obtain the leave of the court in a separate preliminary hearing.

Grounds for an appeal to the High Court

An appeal can only be brought on a point of law, and the court will not interfere with or reinterpret issues of fact.

Effect of an appeal to the High Court on the enforcement notice

If leave is granted to bring the appeal, the effect is not automatically to suspend the enforcement notice until the outcome of the appeal is known, because the court may order that it shall be partially or wholly effective pending the outcome of High Court proceedings.

If an appeal is successful, the effect is to remit the matter to the Secretary of State for reconsideration and redetermination.

Appeals to the High Court are potentially expensive, as an unsuccessful appellant is likely to have to pay the costs of the other party or parties. Specialist legal advice should be sought by anyone contemplating an appeal against an inspector's decision to uphold an enforcement notice.

8

Breaches of Planning Control – Stop Notices and Injunctions

Enforcement proceedings, while effective in the long term, can be time consuming and a long drawn out way of putting a stop to a breach of planning control. If the party on whom the enforcement notice is served appeals to the Secretary of State, it can be many months before the appeal is scheduled for a hearing. Even if the inspector decides to uphold the notice, it is likely to be six to eight weeks before the decision is notified to the parties. The time by which the notice must be complied with does not begin to run until that date. The time for compliance is likely to be a matter of months, if not a year.

If the party on whom the enforcement notice is served, or the unsuccessful appellant, as the case may be, still fails to comply with the enforcement notice once it has become effective, the LPA may not prosecute for failing to comply until after the date for compliance has expired.

If the effects of the breach of planning control are such as to make a quicker remedy desirable, the LPA has two options for halting the breach – or even a potential breach – more quickly. However, the LPA will not automatically do so in every case because there are certain constraints on the use of this power.

Stop notices

In some cases the LPA may wish to put an immediate stop to a breach of planning control, even if it has already served an enforcement notice. If the enforcement notice has not yet taken effect, the LPA may serve a stop notice.

This requires the person on whom the enforcement notice was served to cease some or all of the activities subject of the enforcement notice immediately. The LPA may serve a stop notice even before an enforcement notice comes into effect or even if the party on whom the stop notice is served is appealing to the Secretary of State.

The stop notice must specify the date it takes effect, which will be between 3 and 28 days of service. It cannot be contravened before it takes effect. The reason stop notices are effective is that failure to comply with them once they come into effect is a criminal offence punishable by a fine of up to £20,000 if convicted by magistrates, and a fine at the court's discretion if convicted by the crown court.

The drawback with stop notices is that a criminal prosecution may be required to enforce them, and this is of itself time consuming.

There is no right of appeal to the Secretary of State against stop notices, but in some circumstances the party on whom the stop notice was served may be able to claim compensation from the LPA.

If the appellant's appeal to the Secretary of State against an enforcement notice is successful and results in the enforcement notice being quashed, or if for some other reason the LPA decides to withdraw the enforcement notice, the party on whom the stop notice was served may claim against the LPA for any loss or damage, including loss for breach of contract, which is attributable to the LPA's having prohibited activities which were the subject of the stop notice.

It is this potential liability to pay compensation which tends to restrain the LPA from serving stop notices unless it seems absolutely necessary to do so. Government policy guidance to LPAs on the serving of stop notices is that LPAs should weigh up the public benefit accruing from the serving of the stop notice against the potential liability as to the cost of compensation if the notice was excessive. LPAs will therefore balance these factors carefully before exercising their discretion to issue a stop notice. They will consider what the effects on the local environment and amenity of serving or not serving a stop notice, and how many people are likely to benefit.

Anyone who is affected by the breach of planning control which led to the serving of an enforcement notice, and who is adversely affected by the activities on the land the enforcement notice relates to, can ask the LPA whether it intends to serve a stop notice.

Since the LPA are unlikely to serve a stop notice unless it appears in the public interest to do so, anyone who feels the effects of the breach are sufficient to warrant a stop notice should write to the enforcement officer at the LPA, with a copy to local councillors, pointing out how they are affected by the breach of planning control and why a stop notice ought to be served.

If the LPA must justify an exercise of discretion to serve a stop notice, it is much easier to justify if there is evidence of local pressure to deal with a breach of planning control in this way.

Injunctions

Arguably this is the most drastic power available to the LPA, as it can be used to put a stop not only to breaches of planning control which have already taken place, but to 'apprehended' breaches of control. It is much quicker than other options for enforcing against breaches of planning control, can require immediate compliance and attract immediate criminal liability for a failure to comply.

It can be used whether or not the LPA has exercised any other enforcement powers. It is a particularly useful weapon against persistent offenders, who might otherwise exploit the delay inherent in other methods of planning control.

The LPA must only consider whether it is 'expedient and necessary' to apply for an injunction in the circumstances.

The LPA is only likely to seek an injunction if it seems expedient and necessary as a last resort. In some cases it will depend on the circumstances whether it is expedient and necessary to restrain a party from carrying out activities subject to enforcement proceedings, whether or not an appeal is pending, before the time has elapsed for compliance, and thus obviously before it is known whether criminal proceedings will have to be brought for failure to comply with an enforcement notice.

The LPA does not have to have exercised, or indeed plan to exercise, any of its other powers of enforcement. It may seek an injunction as a permanent measure to prevent an existing breach of control or one the LPA have reason to believe will take place. The problem with this is that in some cases it will be difficult to establish this until the other options for enforcement have been proved not to be effective.

However, the difficulty with injunctions is that even if the LPA is persuaded that an injunction is a necessary step, it does not automatically follow that the court will grant one. The LPA will probably have to persuade the court that the use of its other statutory powers alone would be insufficient to prevent the breach. The law on the granting of injunctions to prevent existing or apprehended breaches of planning control is complex and will depend on individual circumstances in each case.

A temporary injunction may be sought as an instant short term measure to restrain breaches or apprehended breaches of planning control, pending the outcome of a full hearing on a permanent injunction or pending the outcome of other enforcement proceedings.

This use of an injunction as an interim measure is known as an 'interlocutory injunction'. However, if the LPA seeks and obtains an interlocutory injunction, it will have to give an undertaking to the court that if the injunction was wrong, or if the party against whom it is sought later succeeds in the substantive proceedings – for example, a successful appeal to the Secretary of State against an enforcement notice, or a full hearing on the merits of granting a permanent injunction – the LPA will pay compensation for any loss or damage suffered by the party restrained by the injunction.

The undertaking as to damages may be substantial if, for example, the breach of planning control involves the operation of a business of some sort.

If the LPA obtain an injunction, a failure to comply is contempt of court and an offence.

9

Listed Buildings, Conservation Areas and Other Special Cases

An important function of the planning system is the role it plays in protecting and conserving the historic architectural environment.
   It does this by

(i)   identifying those buildings and areas worthy of protection, known respectively as 'listed buildings' and 'conservation areas',

(ii)   applying special controls to development or other works affecting these buildings and areas, once designated, and

(iii) further protection through the use of criminal sanctions to enforce controls and ensure they are maintained and conserved.

   We return to the planning cake analogy.

The legal element

In the case of listed buildings and conservation areas, the legal element of the cake is the 1990 Planning (Listed Buildings and Conservation Areas) Act. This Act provides for the designation of historic buildings or areas of special architectural or historic importance either by 'listing' the buildings or designating an area as a 'conservation area'.
   'Listing' means quite literally that an historic or architecturally

important building is put on a 'list' of such buildings by the DoE. Once listed, the Act provides for special limitations, restrictions and considerations which must apply before the listed building can be demolished or altered, or any development can take place which affects the listed building or its setting.

The Act provides for similar restrictions on development in areas designated as 'conservation areas'. It also provides special powers for LPAs to ensure the protection and maintenance of listed buildings, and, to a lesser extent, to preserve the character and appearance of conservation areas.

The Act enforces the proper application of such controls through criminal sanctions. Under S.9 of the Act, is a criminal offence to execute or cause to be executed any work to demolish a listed building, or to alter or extend a listed building in such as way as to affect its character or the features which had caused it to be listed unless that work has been sanction by listed building consent.

A valid listed building consent may only be granted by the LPA or the Secretary of State and must be in writing.

However, works of demolition or alteration, etc., may be retroactively authorized by the LPA or the Secretary of State. If so, that means they are lawful as from the date such consent is retroactively granted.

Anyone carrying out unauthorized works of demolition, alteration, etc., is guilty of an offence. The only defences are that:

- the works were necessary on grounds of safety, health or to preserve the building;
- temporary works of a more limited nature were not sufficient to safeguard health, safety or the preservation of the building;
- the unauthorized works carried out were the minimum necessary in the circumstances, and
- written notice of the necessity for the works was supplied to the LPA as soon as reasonably practicable.

Failing these grounds of defence, anyone convicted of unauthorized works to a listed building in the magistrates' court is liable to a term of up to six months in prison and/or a fine not exceeding £20,000. If convicted by a jury in the crown court, the penalties are imprisonment for up to two years and/or a fine at the court's discretion.

Central government policy

Central government policy on listed buildings and conservation areas is to be found in Planning Policy Guidance (PPG) 15, 'Planning and the Historic Environment'.

Public consultation

Finally, public consultation plays an increasingly important role in issues involving listed buildings and conservation areas. There is a growing public awareness that modern society's demand for new types of development – in particular major development projects such as motorways, airports, shopping malls, etc. – must be balanced against the public interest in the preservation of the environment, both built and natural. Listed buildings and conservation areas are an extremely important feature of the environment.

Listed buildings

How they are designated

A list of buildings of special architectural or historic importance is kept by the DoE. This list may be added to periodically by the Secretary of State. Normally the procedure for listing involves the Historic Buildings and Monuments Commission (commonly known as English Heritage) preparing lists of buildings suitable for the protection extended by the 1990 Planning (Listed Buildings and Conservation Areas) Act (hereafter referred to as the Listed Buildings Act).

Periodically, most LPAs review the position with regard to listed buildings in their area. The development plan must include policies on conservation in the area, and the protection of the historic environment will feature largely in these policies.

The listed building list is continually being updated and is by no means closed. Normally the listing procedure involves the LPA's bringing a particular building or group of buildings to the attention of English Heritage. In some cases this is the result of lobbying by individuals or interest groups who believe a particular building or group of buildings deserve listed status.

English Heritage have a legal right to enter and inspect buildings, and if they believe any deserves the protection conferred by the listing process, they will include it or them in the list of buildings it submits from time to time to the Secretary of State. However, other persons or bodies of persons may also submit a list or lists of buildings to the Secretary of State.

These other persons or bodies of persons can be almost anyone who has taken an interest, but in view of the powers to enter and inspect which are available to English Heritage but not to the public at large, it may make sense for other parties to approach English Heritage in the first instance to ask if English Heritage will investigate. Alternatively, they may approach the LPA to persuade the LPA to ask English Heritage to investigate.

Classification

Listed buildings are classified in one of three ways: Grade I buildings are of exceptional interest and comprise around 2 per cent of the list. Grade II buildings are those of special interest, and Grade II* designates particularly important buildings in the second category.

Criteria for listing

There are a number of criteria for listing a building. These include:

- the intrinsic architectural and historic importance of the building;
- its rarity;
- particular interior or exterior features;

- the setting of the building;
- its architectural and historical relationship to nearby buildings or groups of building.

These criteria do not necessarily depend on architectural merit. A building may be of special architectural or historic importance because it represents a certain type of building typical of its time, because there are particular historic associations with the building, or because of its value as part of a group of buildings. Sometimes the architectural or historic interest which justified its listed status lies at the core of the building and has been concealed by later development.

The Secretary of State may either approve the list, amend the list or approve it with modifications. Before doing so he or she must consult both English Heritage and any other experts who appear to have relevant special knowledge of the buildings in question.

What features are 'listed'

Occasionally questions arise about the effect of listing in a particular case, or to what part or features of a particular building does the listing process extend. Whether a feature of a listed building is comprehended in the 'listing' is important because in some cases, seemingly minor works or alterations to features of a listed building, which would not normally amount to 'development' within the terms of the Town and Country Planning Act will nevertheless affect something which is listed and therefore requires listed building consent before it can proceed lawfully.

Listing confers protection on any object or structure fixed to the building, and can include both interior and exterior features like original panelling, staircases, windows, carvings, etc. Listing also confers protection on any object or structure within the curtilage of the building which forms part of the land on which the building is situated, and which has been within the curtilage of the building since 1 July 1948. This means that a stable block, garden wall, swimming pool, outbuildings, etc., may also be listed if part of the site of the listed building since 1948.

There is a large body of case law on the subject of what structures are attached to a building or within its curtilage, and broadly speaking the position is that it will be a matter of fact, degree and history in any given case.

Anyone contemplating development in any form to a listed building, and who is unsure whether listed building consent is required, should check with the LPA first.

Temporary listing

This is an emergency measure available to the LPA to protect a building which is of special architectural or historic significance, which is not yet listed, and which is in immediate danger of demolition or alteration which might affect its special historic features.

In such a situation the LPA may serve a building preservation notice informing the owner or occupier that the building appears to be of special architectural importance and that the LPA has requested the Secretary of State to include it in the list of such buildings. The effect is to confer the immediate protection of the 1990 Act for a brief period.

Urgent cases

In very urgent cases where the delay of serving the notice on the owner or occupier might take too long – for example if a building appears to be at risk of immediate demolition – the LPA may simply affix the building preservation notice to a conspicuous place on the building. It is of immediate effect, and demolition or any works to the building cannot lawfully be carried out without going through all the proper procedures in the Listed Buildings Act. Anyone who carries out unlawful work to a listed butting commits a criminal offence.

However, building preservation notices are of limited duration and expire after six months. During that time the Secretary of State may either list the building, refuse to list the building, or fail to take any decision. If the Secretary of State notifies the LPA that he does not intend to list the building, the LPA is prohibited from serving another building preservation notice for 12 months from the date of such notification.

If the building is listed by the Secretary of State, the Listed Buildings Act continues to apply. If not, the notice and the temporary protection lapse together. If the Secretary of State takes no action by the end of the six month period, the notice lapses and the building is once again subject only to normal planning controls (under the 1990 Town and Country Planning Act).

Special controls on development of listed buildings

The Listed Buildings Act does not prevent all development to listed buildings. If it did so it is likely many would simply collapse as their existence could not be economically extended. It is often the case that a listed building can be most effectively preserved if given a new lease on life by sensitive redevelopment.

The Listed Buildings Act provides for an extra degree of control to be exercised by the LPA, who must grant consent for any works to or development of a listed building which demolish, extend or alter the building in any manner affecting its historical character or features of architectural interest (which led it to be listed in the first place). This includes works to or development which might affect any of the interior or exterior features of the building or which are within the curtilage of the building.

The Act requires that anyone proposing to carry out such works must first make an application for listed building consent from the LPA. This is in addition to any planning permission that may be necessary in the circumstances. Alternatively, it may be that while no planning permission is required for development or change of use, listed building consent is required on its own.

Anyone proposing to demolish a listed building must obtain consent from both the LPA and English Heritage.

APPLICATION FOR
LISTED BUILDING OR
CONSERVATION AREA CONSENT

For Office Use Only

App. No. | | | | | | | | | | |

You should use this form for applying for consent for:-
- Alterations and/or extensions to Listed Buildings
- Demolition or part demolition of Listed Buildings
- Demolition or part demolition of Unlisted Buildings in a Conservation Area

Different forms are available for all other types of planning application from Planning Transport & Development

PLEASE READ THE ACCOMPANYING NOTES BEFORE COMPLETING THIS FORM
PLEASE COMPLETE THE FORM IN BLOCK CAPITALS
PLEASE GIVE ALL MEASUREMENTS IN METRIC

1. Name and Address of Applicant

Name...

Address..

....

....

....

....

Postcode..

Daytime Tel. No...................................

2. Name and Address of Agent *(if completed by Agent)*

Name...

Address..

....

....

Postcode..

Contact Name......................................

Daytime Tel. No...................................

3. Full Postal Address of the building(s) which are to be altered/extended/demolished

....

.... Postcode.................

4. Detailed Description of Proposed Works including external materials

....

....

....

....

continue on separate sheet

Figure 6 Application form for listed building or conservation area consent

5. Type of Application

The proposal involves:-

Please tick

a. Total demolition of a Listed Building or detached outbuildings of a Listed Building a

b. Demoltion of part of a Listed Building (also complete Q6) b

c. Alterations to the interior of a Listed Building c

d. Alterations to the exterior of a Listed Building d

e. Extension of a Listed Building e

f. Remove or vary a Condition f

g. Demolition of a unlisted building in a Conservation Area (also complete Q6) g

Please complete if relevant

6. The proposal involves the demolition of all or part of the building, and is required for the following reasons:

....

....

....

7. Previous or Concurrent Planning Applications

Please tick

a. I have already been granted planning permission for this proposal a

b. I have already applies for planning permission for this proposal b

c. I am applying concurrently for planning permission c

d. Planning permission is not required for proposed works d

If you have ticked a or b, please state Application No. W

8. **Please give details (Date, Source, Amount) of any grants made from public funds for the repair or maintenance of the building**

....

....

continue on separate sheet if necessary

CHECKLIST

Please tick

A 6 copies of this form, signed and dated

B 6 copies of the Certificate of Ownership, signed and dated

C 6 copies of scaled plans

 (i) the location/site plan with application site outlined in red. Any other land the applicant's ownership or under the control of the applicant should be edged in blue.

 (ii) the block/layout plan showing the position of adjoining land and buildings

 (iii) floor plans and elevations

D If the proposal involves the demolition or part demolition of a listed building the Council is required to notify the additional independent bodies and consequently it will be helpful if an extra 6 copies of each drawing are submitted in these cases.

- This form only concerns listed building or conservation area consent.
- It is likely that you will also require planning or advertisement approval. Please contact the Planning and Transport Development Department if you are in any doubt.
- Most building work also needs separate approval under the Building Regulations. Please contact the Council's Building Control Section in the Planning Department to find out if approval is needed.

Signed ....(Applicant/Agent) Date ....

Figure 6 Application form for listed building or conservation area consent (Continued)

Listed building consent procedure

This is similar to an application for planning permission. The appropriate form is obtainable from the LPA. The application for consent must specify clearly the building which is subject of the application, and must be accompanied by such plans and drawings as are necessary to describe the works for which consent is sought.

The application must be accompanied by the appropriate ownership certificate, indicating whether the applicant owns the listed building and if not, who does and whether they have been duly notified of the application.

Outside of London, LPAs have a duty to notify the Secretary of State of applications for listed building consent.

Inside London, London borough councils must notify English Heritage of any applications for listed building consent unless the LPA is minded to refuse the application.

The Secretary of State has power to 'call in' an application for listed building consent to be dealt with by him in the first instance. In such cases the Secretary of State will hold a public inquiry if either the applicant or the LPA so wish, before determining the matter.

Applications for listed building consent must be advertised, and notices posted in the same way as applies to applications for planning permission (except for applications for consent applying to only to interior works on a Grade II building). The purpose, as with public notification of planning applications, is to allow third parties an opportunity to make representations to the LPA about the application for listed building consent.

The statutory duty of the LPA or, as may be, the Secretary of State, in determining applications under the Listed Buildings Act is to have special regard to the desirability of preserving the building or its setting or any features of special architectural or historic interest which it possesses. (Note that this is a different duty from the one which applies to applications for planning permission, requiring the LPA to 'have regard to the provisions of the development plan and all material considerations' under the Town and Country Planning Act.)

The development plan must provide for policies to protect the environment, and although the statutory duty in respect of listed buildings applications does not specify what regard must be had to those policies, clearly they will be taken into account when the LPA consider the application. It would be difficult for the LPA to pay 'special regard' to the 'desirability' of preserving the building, its setting or features in the absence of regard to development plan policies on conservation.

An applicant for listed building consent, and any third parties, should therefore acquaint themselves with the relevant development plan policies in the same way and for the same reasons they would do so in respect of planning applications.

Government policy advice: PPG 15, 'Planning and the Historic Environment'

Anyone concerned with an application for listed building consent should refer to this policy document, as it sets out quite fully central government's policy on listed buildings and conservation areas, and the application of the special development controls which apply in these cases.

The thrust of the policy advice is the necessity for a balancing of the issues involved in listed building consent applications. Any applicant or third party will probably wish to emphasize various elements of this policy advice to the LPA, depending on whether the party in question is supporting or objecting to the application.

The LPA or the Secretary of State may either grant or refuse listed building consent, or grant it subject to conditions.

Power of the LPA to revoke or modify any consent granted

Even if the LPA grants consent, it is possible for this consent to be revoked or modified at a later stage. However, this requires a formal order, which must be confirmed by the Secretary of State.

The procedure for such an order, if contested by any party seeking to implement the consent, may involve a public inquiry.

If the LPA later revokes or modifies a consent, any person with an interest in the building may have a claim for compensation against the LPA for expenditure incurred in implementing or partially implementing the consent, or any other loss or damage which has resulted directly from the revocation or modification.

As to modification, the consent may only be modified in respect of any part of the consent which has not yet been implemented.

Right of appeal against refusal of listed building consent, conditions attached to any consent granted, or non-determination of the application

If the LPA refuses consent or fails to determine an application within the statutory eight-week period, the applicant has a right of appeal to the Secretary of State (in the same way there is a right of appeal against refusal of planning permission or failure to determine an such an application).

The appeal must be brought within six months of notification of the LPA's decision. The appeal form is available from the DoE. The appellant must furnish the Secretary of State with:

- a copy of the application for listed building consent;
- all relevant maps, plans and drawings;
- a copy of the ownership certificate
- copies of all correspondence with the LPA relating to the application.

Grounds of appeal

The notice of appeal must set out the grounds of appeal. These grounds may include a claim that the building is wrongly listed because it is not of sufficiently special historic or architectural interest, and that it ought to be removed from the list. In cases where a building preservation notice has been served, it is likewise a ground of appeal that on its architectural and historic merits, the building ought not to be listed.

The applicant may also appeal against any conditions attached to the consent. As with appeals against the refusal of planning permission or non-determination of applications, etc., appeals against refusal. etc. of listed building consent may be by way of written representations or, at the request of either the appellant or the LPA, a public inquiry. The procedural rules governing listed building consent public inquiries are the same as those governing planning inquiries. Appellants and third parties should prepare their cases accordingly (see Chapters 3, 4 and 5).

Anyone giving evidence or making representations by letter, either at the application for consent stage or at the appeal stage, is advised to refer to PPG 15. This policy document can provide helpful guidance in making the case for or against the listed building consent.

The inspector may be assisted at the appeal by a specialist assessor or independent expert.

In appeals involving development to Grade I and Grade II* buildings, the appeal will be determined by the Secretary of State. Appeals involving Grade II buildings will normally be determined by the inspector. The Secretary of State or the inspector have power to refuse or allow the appeal, or allow it subject to conditions. There is also power to remove buildings from the list on such appeals.

As with planning appeals, any 'person aggrieved' by the decision of the inspector or the Secretary of State may appeal to the High Court on the grounds that the decision is outside the powers of the act, or that the relevant requirements have not been complied with (see Chapter 6, Appeals to the High Court).

Remedies available when listed building consent is refused or granted subject to impracticable conditions

In some cases the owner of a listed building may metaphorically throw up his or her hands in despair if unable to obtain listed building consent, or if the consent obtained is subject to conditions which are difficult, too expensive or impracticable to comply with. If so, the owner may be able to serve a listed building purchase notice on the LPA, effectively requiring the LPA to buy the listed building.

The necessary preconditions for service of a listed buildings purchase notice are:

- listed building consent has been refused/revoked/modified or granted subject to conditions, and
- the building and land in their present state are not capable of reasonably beneficial use as a result of the refusal/ revocation/modification or conditions.

The major problem with this procedure from the owner's point of view, is that the question of what constitutes 'reasonably beneficial use' is a difficult one, and depends very much on individual circumstances of the building and the land attached to it.

The LPA is not required to purchase the listed building unless it 'accepts' the notice or the Secretary of State confirms it. If the LPA rejects the notice, it is referred to the Secretary of State who may confirm or amend the notice to take affect in such a way as he or she shall direct. He may also order a public inquiry to be held before determining whether or to what extent to confirm the notice.

Enforcement action

As with breaches of planning control, the LPA may take enforcement action in respect of unauthorized works to a listed building if it appears expedient to it to do so. These breaches include carrying out development without compliance with any conditions attached to a listed building consent.

The LPA may require the building to be restored to its former state. If that is not practicable, it may require the person on whom the enforcement notice is served to carry out such further works as may be necessary to alleviate the effects of the unauthorized works, or it may require the person to carry out works which bring the development of the building into line with the terms of any listed building consent, conditional or not, which has been granted.

Unauthorized works to a listed building include its demolition.

There is a right of appeal to the Secretary of State against an enforcement notice, which is similar to the proceedings which apply in respect of a planning enforcement notice. The procedure is regulated partly by Schedule 3 of the Act and partly by the Town and Country Planning (Enforcement Notices and Appeals) Regulations 1991. The appeal must be made to the Secretary of State before the date the notice comes into effect. The appeal may be by way of written representations or by way of public inquiry.

The grounds of appeal are:

- the building subject of the notice is not one of special interest;
- there has been no breach of listed building control as alleged in the notice;
- the works alleged to constitute unauthorized development to the listed building were urgently necessary;
- listed building consent ought in any case to be granted for the works;
- the listed building enforcement notice was not properly served.

As with planning enforcement appeals, the appeal must be advertised and notified to the public. Written statement of the grounds of appeal must be submitted to the Secretary of State, and otherwise similar provision about serving of statements of case by other interested parties apply. Any third party wishing to make representations either by letter or in person at the inquiry may notify the Secretary of State accordingly.

Procedure at the inquiry is the same as in other enforcement appeals, or indeed most other public inquiries. The Secretary of State may uphold or quash the enforcement notice, may vary it or may grant listed building consent for all or part of the unauthorized development subject of the notice. He may discharge conditions subject to which listed building consent was granted, or may remove the building's listed status.

If an enforcement notice becomes affective because it is not appealed, or if the Secretary of State upholds the notice, failure to comply with it is a criminal offence punishable by a fine up to £20,000 in the magistrates' court and a fine at the judge's discretion in the crown court.

The decision of the Secretary of State on a listed building enforcement notice may be challenged in the High Court on point of law.

Other powers of the LPA to protect and maintain listed buildings

If a listed building has fallen into disrepair the LPA or the Secretary of State may serve a notice of repair on the owner, requiring him or her to carry out such works as are necessary. If that is insufficient to ensure restorative works are carried out by the owner, the LPA and the Secretary of State have powers to compulsorily acquire a listed building in need of repair.

Compensation to the owner will be determined by the Lands Tribunal. If the owner has deliberately allowed the building to deteriorate, minimum compensation will be payable. If the listed building has been demolished, the Secretary of State or the LPA may compulsorily purchase the site. Alternatively, if it appears to the LPA that urgent works are necessary to preserve a listed building, the LPA may carry out the works and recover the cost from the owner. However, LPAs also have powers to make grants or contributions to the cost of preserving listed buildings.

The exercise of the various powers available to protect

listed buildings will depend very much on the facts and circumstances of each individual case. Any third party, whether a single individual or an organization, can request the LPA or the Secretary of State to act in the case of a listed building which appears to be at risk, through disrepair or unauthorized development.

Applications for development affecting the setting of a listed building

Considerations about the effect of development on listed buildings can arise even when the application is for development or change of use under the Planning Act. Aside from the requirement for listed building consent, the Listed Buildings Act also recognizes that applications for planning permission may also have an effect on nearby listed buildings. The wider setting of listed buildings can be extremely important, and relevant to their character, appearance and historical or architectural value.

If it appears to the LPA that a planning application affects the setting of a listed building, that application must be advertised to that effect in a local newspaper and a site notice must be posted. In most cases, the application must also be notified to English Heritage.

Conservation areas

These are areas identified by LPAs as being of special historic or architectural interest. The Listed Buildings Act operates to provide controls on development within and affecting conservation areas. Conservation areas may or may not include listed buildings, and are significant in their own right. In many cases there will be an overlap between the controls imposed on listed buildings and those in conservation areas, as many conservation areas contain listed buildings.

However, the controls on listed buildings are far more stringent, and if listed building consent is necessary, it will usually render conservation area consent unnecessary.

Conservation area consent is only required for demolition of any building, including some structures such as garden walls, in a conservation area. LPAs must consider the effects of that demolition on the character and appearance of the conservation area, and whether or not it is desirable to conserve or enhance that character or appearance in determining such applications. Otherwise, planning permission for development in a conservation area must be sought for a new development or a change of use in the usual way.

How conservation areas are designated

LPAs should periodically review the position on conservation areas within their boroughs, and consider whether any further areas ought to be designated. The Secretary of State also has powers to designate conservation areas if it appears to him an area is one of special architectural or historical significance and it is desirable to preserve or enhance its character or appearance.

Once an area is designated, buildings within it cannot be demolished and trees cannot be cut down, lopped, damaged or destroyed without conservation area consent. Any planning applications which would be likely to affect the special historic or architectural character of the area must be advertised as to that effect, to allow the public an opportunity to comment on the proposal in light of its effect on the conservation area.

Permitted development rights under the General Development Order are restricted in conservation areas. Thus anyone proposing to carry out even minor development in a conservation area is advised to check with the LPA first to see if planning permission is necessary.

The Conservation Area Code

This is an appendix to the Listed Buildings Act and to a large extent mirrors the provisions of the Act which apply to listed buildings, including powers of enforcement and appeals, etc.

However, what requires conservation area consent is demolition of a building in the conservation area. Conservation area consent is not required for works to a building in a conservation area. For those, a planning application must be submitted in accordance with the requirements of the 1990 Town and Country Planning Act.

Effect of designation

Aside from the circumstances in which conservation area consent is required, one of the main effects of designation as a conservation area is that when the LPA determines an application for planning permission under the 1990 Planning Act, the Listed Buildings Act requires them to have regard to the desirability of preserving and enhancing the character and appearance of the conservation area as a material consideration.

Thus anyone proposing to seek planning permission for development or a change of use in a conservation area should bear this test in mind and would be well advised to consult the LPA in advance of submitting the application. There may be precedents for similar development in the conservation area which are useful, and it should be possible to see what is or is not acceptable in principle to the LPA.

Potential developers can encounter stiff local opposition to development in conservation areas, which may (and frequently does) result in an active local campaign to persuade the LPA that the development is unsuitable in the conservation area. This can lead to the application being refused, with the attendant alternatives (and cost) of abandoning the application, amending and re-submitting the application or going to appeal.

The LPA – and the Secretary of State and his inspectors – will subject applications in such sensitive areas to very close scrutiny indeed. It is therefore a sensible precaution for an intending developer to consider how the impact of the proposal is likely to be viewed, and how potential objections, both from the LPA and third parties, might be overcome, before submitting the application.

Applications for conservation area consent

The same advice applies to applications for conservation area consent to demolish a building in a conservation area. Anyone applying for this can expect that local feelings on demolition even of unlisted buildings can run high.

Even where a building is unsightly, in poor repair or incapable of use, there may be a body of opinion in favour of preserving it simply because it is part of the conservation area, and people are wary about the impact of anything which might be built in its place.

Once again, it is sensible to identify what such concerns might be in advance. Intending developers should remember that others may not appreciate the aesthetic or economic benefits of the proposal quite as thoroughly as do the developers themselves. Even seemingly innocuous proposals can arouse storms of protest. It may not be possible to eliminate all potential objections, but a clearly thought out application is likely to encounter fewer obstacles.

Other special cases

Special material considerations apply if a development proposal affects land in a green belt, an area of outstanding natural beauty, or an ancient monument. These considerations apply to confer the extra protection necessary to ensure their preservation, and to prevent their being unduly or inappropriately affected by the development process.

(i) Green belts

Green belts are defined by their name. It is, and has been for many years, government policy that 'belts' of green (i.e. rural) land be identified in development plans to serve the following purposes:

- to contain urban sprawl;
- to protect the countryside from encroaching development;
- to preserve the individual nature of towns and prevent their merging into each other;
- to ensure that the special historic character of towns is not lost to developmental encroachment;
- to promote the process of urban regeneration;
- to retain areas of rural countryside for the benefit of the general public.

Green belts are intended to be of a permanent nature in order to fullfil their functions, and there is a strong presumption against 'inappropriate' development in green belts.

It is government policy that new building within green belts should rarely be given planning approval, and that such development as is permitted by LPAs should generally be limited to proposals for the re-use of existing buildings for a limited range of activities typical of the countryside. These include agriculture, forestry, sport, or cemeteries.

It is also government policy that the visual impact of any proposal for development in a green belt, even if within the limited categories which might be acceptable in principle, must not have an intrusive visual impact.

While every planning application must be considered on its merits, would-be developers applying for planning permission may find it extremely difficult to obtain. If the area contains a green belt, development plan policies are likely to echo central government policy restrictions on development, and may even contain further restrictions.

As a general rule of thumb, developers should be aware that unless the application for development in a green belt is particularly well thought out in advance, the risk of refusal is very high.

Anyone intending to seek planning permission for development or a change of use in a green belt should first refer to Planning Policy Guidance (PPG) 2 on green belts, and consider whether the development proposal can be considered in line with the policy guidelines. It is, as always, advisable to consult the LPA to see what the development plan says about green belts, and whether there are any policies qualifying the general restrictions. If so, it may be that the proposed scheme can be tailored to comply with such policies. This is a point which ought to be discussed with the planning department before submitting the application.

Similarly, any third parties concerned about green belt development ought to acquaint themselves with PPG 2 and the development plan, and make their case for or against the proposal to the LPA accordingly.

Areas of outstanding natural beauty

AONBs are designated by the Countryside Commission and at present make up approximately 13 per cent of the total land area of England and Wales. Once an area is designated, it is government policy that development controls should apply to preserve its beauty. Individual development plans will contain specific policies about development in AONBs within their areas. These policies should be directed at the preservation of the special landscape features of the AONB.

There are restrictions on permitted development rights under the General Development Order in AONBs, but small-scale, appropriately designed development to meet the needs of residents of local communities is acceptable in principle. Policy considerations recognize that a balance needs to be struck between the necessity of preserving the AONB, and the necessity for maintaining the local rural economy.

Anyone intending to apply for planning permission should consult Policy Planning Guidance (PPG) 7 on 'The Countryside and the Rural Economy' and ensure that an environmental impact assessment study accompanies the application (see Chapter 11). It is advisable to consult with the LPA on the proposal to see what development policies apply, whether in principle the proposal is acceptable, and whether amendments to the scheme are possible to meet any potential objections.

Anyone wishing to make representations for or against the proposal should also take the relevant policies in the development plan and PPG 7 into account when making their representations to the LPA.

Ancient monuments

Ancient monuments are sites of particular national importance which qualify for special protection because they are typical of a certain period, have unusual features, are a rarity, are fragile or are documented in contemporary historical records. There are approximately 13,000 sites on a schedule specifying them as ancient monuments. Once a monument is scheduled, certain controls apply with respect to any developmental works which might affect it. Any proposal likely to demolish, destroy, damage or affect an ancient monument in almost any way requires the consent of the Secretary of State.

Further information about ancient monument consents is available from the Department of the Environment (Heritage Division).

LPAs will only consider planning applications for works likely to affect ancient monuments if submitted with detailed plans. If a planning application is made for works which will affect the setting of an ancient monument, this will be a material consideration in determining the application.

Areas of archaeological importance

There are at present five such designated areas: the town centres of Chester, Canterbury, York, Exeter and Hereford. Anyone proposing to carry out development for which permission has been granted in these areas must notify the LPA if intending to flood, tip on or disturb the land. Investigations may then be carried out by a body appointed by the Secretary of State, who may investigate and if necessary, excavate the site for up to four and a half months prior to development works being allowed to proceed.

Archaeological remains which surface in the course of development works

Such an unforeseen event can cause considerable problems for a developer if work must be halted to consider the best way of dealing with these remains. If the LPA or objectors to the proposal have any evidence of archaeological remains on the development site, it may be worth the developer looking very closely at this information or even investigating further before going ahead.

At the very least, the discovery of archaeological remains can hold up development works while investigations are undertaken as to their extent, importance, and the further steps which may be necessary to protect them.

The Secretary of State may decide they should be added to the schedule of ancient monuments if appropriate, or other steps may need to be taken to safeguard them. There is potential for a real and costly conflict between the interests of the developer and the interests of archaeology. English Heritage may be able to assist the developer and they should be consulted in such an eventuality.

A developer who has reason to suspect archaeological remains might be present on the development site or uncovered in the course of construction works should consider insuring against the cost of delay if they are discovered.

Acacia road residents association let it be known that
they objected to the ministry's development proposal

10

Development by the Crown

This involves a variation of the planning system cake.

The Crown – bodies such as the Ministry of Defence, Crown Estates, the Home Office, the Metropolitan Police, etc. – controls a great deal of land on which, from time to time, development will be carried out. It is a widely held belief that in planning matters, the Crown is 'above the law' and therefore the public is denied the normal consultation process.

While there is some justification for that view, in practice it is not wholly true. The Crown are always exempt from legislation unless the legislation specifically provides they are not, and Crown bodies are not subject either to the 1990 Town and Country Planning Act or the 1990 Listed Buildings Act.

However, this exemption from the law only applies to the Crown. It does not apply to any tenants of the Crown, or persons having some subsidiary interest in the property. Crown Estate leaseholders would be an example. While the Crown Estate may carry out development on its land or alter or demolish listed buildings, for example, without attracting penalties or being subjected to enforcement proceedings, Crown Estate tenants may not.

They, like everyone else, are subject to the planning legislation, and may not themselves carry out development or alter listed buildings without following normal procedures to obtain the appropriate consents.

'Policy' controls: how effective are they?

However, although planning law does not apply to Crown bodies, as a matter of government policy, set out in DoE Circular 18/84, 'Crown Land and Crown Development', Crown bodies should follow non-statutory consultation procedures when proposing to carry out development. These are very similar to the procedures which apply under the Acts. Whether these procedures actually secure effective public consultation, and result in the exercise of any control over Crown development, depends on circumstances and the strength of the representations made, because ultimately, for all practical purposes, there is nothing save the strength of public opinion to stop the Crown proceeding regardless.

Given that the use of 'policy' to control Crown development is something of a grey area, it is particularly important for anyone affected by a Crown proposal to understand how the parallel procedure works and at what points it is sensitive to public pressure.

When a Crown department proposes to carry out development, instead of applying for planning permission, it submits a Notice of Proposed Development to the LPA, including any maps, plans or drawings. The LPA must keep a register of such notices, for public inspection, in the same way as a register is kept for planning applications.

There is no legal requirement for the LPA to advertise the notice in the press and by a site notice, but in practice many will do so as a matter of course, particularly if there is likely to be considerable local response. Any advertisement or site notice will indicate a time within which anyone affected by the development proposal may write to the LPA making representations.

Anyone affected may then inspect the application and plans made available by the LPA as if the Notice of Proposed Development were a planning application.

Normally the LPA must respond to the Crown department in question within eight weeks of receiving the notice. Its response should take into account such representations as have been made, and any views expressed by statutory or amenity bodies. The

LPA must inform the Crown department whether it objects to the proposal or whether there are any conditions the LPA feels should be imposed.

'Urgent' cases

However, there are cases in which the Crown wish to proceed more quickly. In such cases the notice will be specified as being of 'special urgency'. This may have the effect of denying the opportunity for public consultation, as in such cases the LPA is not expected to take any steps to notify the public, and is under pressure to respond to the notice within two weeks.

Many people understandably take a dim view of proposals rushed through in this way. If anyone suspects such a proposal may have been sent to the LPA or is likely to be sent in the foreseeable future, it is advisable to contact local councillors requesting to be kept informed of any Crown notices marked 'special urgency'. If one is received, local residents will need to act quickly to ascertain what the proposal involves and to make their views known to the LPA.

If a Crown proposal conflicts with the policies in the development plan, it should be approached in the same way as planning applications which do so. In such cases, the LPA is obliged by law to apply the policies of the development plan unless there are good reasons for not doing so.

Crown development and the development plan

The LPA must consider the notice having regard to the policies of the development plan and all material considerations (such as local objections).

As discussed before, development plan policies are often

couched in qualified terms, allowing for exceptions to the stated policies. It will be important for objectors to know what development plan policies apply, and to lobby their local councillors as to their proper their application. In the cases of 'special urgency', there is obviously a case to be made that the urgency justifies the qualification allowing the policy to be set aside. Anyone who believes this is inappropriate should respond quickly with representations, but also making the point to the LPA that the 'urgency' may result in denying local residents an opportunity to be consulted.

Most LPAs – whose councillors are after all answerable to the local electorate – will be as helpful as possible to local residents, particularly once they are aware of the strength of local feeling. The notice will be considered by the planning committee of the LPA in the same way as planning applications are considered. Normally local residents may attend these meetings, and in some cases, speak briefly about the proposal.

The LPA must respond to the Crown department indicating whether or not there are objections to the proposal and on what grounds. The Crown will in some cases seek to see if the proposal can be amended or other steps taken to meet these objections. At the end of the day, the issue is whether or not the LPA has unresolved objections to the proposal.

What happens if objections are unresolved?

Three things can happen:

(i) The Crown department can abandon the proposal.
(ii) The Secretary of State may order a non-statutory inquiry. This means that although there is no legal framework for such an inquiry, as a matter of policy he may exercise his discretion to hold one. Needless to say, the exercise of ministerial discretion is often influenced by the strength of public feeling generated by a particular proposal. Depending on the issues involved and the public reaction to the proposal, there may be a case which local people wish to see examined through the public inquiry process. If so, this may become the subject of further lobbying.

(iii)   Because the Crown do not require planning permission – and are immune from enforcement proceedings – at the end of the day there is nothing to stop the Crown going ahead with the proposal regardless of unresolved objections.

Tips on campaigning in respect of a Crown proposal

In view of possibility (iii), those seeking to ensure that their views on Crown development proposals are heard and are as effective as possible should appreciate this may require more time and effort than with matters arising in connection with the planning legislation. In the absence of the force of law, public pressure is the most effective tool available. The following points should prove helpful in mobilizing it:

1.   As with planning applications, it is imperative to begin with a thorough understanding of what is actually being proposed in the notice and any plans. Everyone should be clear about what is proposed, what the impact of the development will be, and how that affects local interests and amenities for better or worse. If in doubt about the impact – for example the size of the proposal – ask if a planning officer can meet with affected residents to answer any questions.

        It is a good idea to see what the planning department's views may be. They may differ from those of the local councillors on the planning committee who will ultimately consider the notice, although the planning officer will make recommendations to the committee.

2.   Any opposition to (or support for) Crown development will be more effective if the objectors or supporters are organized. A body of people speak with a stronger voice than individuals and information and campaigning tasks

can be shared. Some members of the group may be able to provide facilities for photocopying or filing. In some cases a group will need to consider raising funds to meet the cost of campaigning.

3.   It can be helpful to prepare a brief information document setting out what the planning issues are, the likely impact of the proposal, and if appropriate what steps could be taken by the Crown department to address these concerns. It should set out the grounds on which the particular organization object to or support the proposal.

Such a document prepared as soon as possible can be a good way of disseminating information about the proposal to local residents, and provide a good guide to the issues for those who write letters to the LPA. The document can also be sent to local councillors and the press. One or more members of the group can draft this document and someone else may undertake to deal with requests for information and see that it is copied and sent out.

4.   Media involvement plays an important role in highlighting public concerns over Crown development. Often local press or television or radio stations will cover development issues involving a Crown department and local reactions. Depending on the issues involved and the scale of the proposal (and the corresponding reaction), the national press may pick up the story as well.

If a group has been formed, one or two members can act as press officers. They should not be shy about ringing up the press and asking whether someone would be interested in covering the story. They should be able to explain briefly what the story is about, indicate the strength of local opposition or support and the reasons why. They should also make every effort to accommodate the press. If a television station rings at 10 a.m. wanting to send a TV crew round to film the site and /or residents for the midday news, it is no good asking if next Thursday, or even later that day, would be convenient. There will be another story by that time.

It is also useful to think in terms of sound bites about what makes a planning story interesting when approaching the press. 'Local Outrage Over Threat of Concrete Bunker Development in Conservation Areas' is a more enticing title for a press article than 'Government to Build Building'. It is also helpful to be well prepared with all relevant information. The press will always contact the other party or parties involved in a story, and it may be possible to anticipate their response and tell the press how the action group views the likely response.

5. The group should lobby their own councillors and those on the planning committee about sustaining objections or supporting the proposal. There is no reason they should not at the same time lobby the relevant government department and the minister concerned. Copies of such letters should be sent to the local MP, with a request for his or her assistance. The press may decide this is a story in its own right.

Media attention is useful in its own right but usually more so when focused on politicians being asked about the development proposal in question. Media scrutiny can produce interesting and sometimes informative responses from the politicians involved. In some cases it is the most effective, if not the only, way for the public to enjoy anything like 'consultation' over a development proposal by the Crown.

'Local residents felt the Environmental Impact Assessment had its shortcomings.

11

Environmental Impact Assessments

The environmental effects, if any, of a development proposal are a material consideration which must be taken into account when determining whether permission ought to be granted. This is true whether permission is sought by way of an application from the LPA, on an appeal to the Secretary of State, or on a deemed application for planning permission in an appeal from an enforcement notice.

However, there are some categories of development which are by their nature likely to have such an impact on the environment that they cannot be considered by the LPA unless the developer submits an environmental impact assessment with the application. An environmental impact assessment, sometimes known as an environmental statement, is a study required by an EEC directive, and enacted in the 1988 Town and Country Planning (Assessment of Environmental Effects) Regulations.

Which projects require environmental assessments?

Whether the LPA requires an environmental assessment depends on whether it comes within one of two categories. The first, set out in Schedule 1 to the Regulations, requires an environmental statement for a range of major development projects such as crude oil refineries, radioactive waste processing, iron and steel works, some installations for the extraction of asbestos, various chemical processing installations, some roads, airports, etc. In cases of Schedule 1 development, an environmental assessment is mandatory.

In the case of applications for the types of development listed in Schedule 2, the LPA will require an environmental assessment if it considers the proposal is of a nature, size and location likely to have significant effects on the environment.

This list includes certain types of agricultural activities, extractive industrial processes, power installations (including wind generators), glass making, infrastructure projects (such as a motorway service stations) etc.

If there is a proposal for Schedule 2 type of development,local residents and amenity societies may well wish to know whether the LPA has in fact required a study to be prepared, and if so what it says. Any study which is prepared will be available on display to the public, together with the application, maps, plans and other supporting documents.

What the environmental assessment contains

The assessment is required by the Regulations to incorporate certain information: broadly speaking this includes a description of the site and proposal, what data has been used to assess the effects of the development on the environment (i.e. likely impact on people, wildlife, nature, water, air, etc.) or the historic environment, including listed buildings and conservation areas, and the likely direct and indirect effects resulting from the use of pollutants on natural resources, etc.

Normally an environmental statement will also include information about any mitigating measures the developer intends to take to minimize harm foreseen by the assessment.

Challenging the environmental assessment

Environmental assessments may seem daunting and sometimes technical to read, but anyone affected by development for which an assessment has been prepared ought to try getting to grips with it. The LPA must be able to understand what it says before it can consider the proposal, and there is no reason not to ask it to explain any terms, technicalities or any part of the study which seems difficult to understand.

It is important to remember that just because an environmental study looks glossy and formidable does not necessarily mean it is accurate. Sometimes people with local knowledge of the area are better placed to perceive environmental consequences in the locality than outside consultants who have prepared the assessment. It is always worth going over the assessment with a fine tooth comb and an open mind.

If information in the assessment is wrong, the conclusions as to the impact of the development will be wrong as well. Careful note should be made of the weaknesses of the assessment and the implications of those weaknesses. Representations about the application can then be made to the LPA accordingly.

People should remember they can sometimes pick up aspects of a proposal which have eluded (or been ignored by) everyone else, the developer and LPA alike, and should not be intimidated from challenging the assessment.

If the proposal goes to an appeal to the Secretary of State and a public inquiry, the developer will almost certainly call whoever prepared the environmental assessment as a witness. If so, anyone who wishes to be heard at the inquiry will be given an opportunity to cross examine such witnesses. Although there is no statutory right to do so, the inspector is unlikely to refuse anyone the opportunity.

Questioning the developer's environmental witness

To use the opportunity to the best advantage, third parties wishing to ask the same questions of environmental witnesses should get together to prepare their questions in advance. It is preferable if one person is appointed as 'advocate' to ask questions and present a case for others with a similar point of view or concerns. The questions or cross examination of specialist witnesses can become very lengthy, and possibly more so in the hands of those who are not professional advocates.

It is not easy to challenge the environmental assessment in an inquiry because they often contain a wealth of technical detail. The following tips will help third parties to do so effectively without irritating the inspector by repetition:

1.   It is imperative that you have studied the assessment thoroughly and know what it says – and does not say. You will feel confident and do a better job as a result.

2.   Prepare the questions you believe are appropriate in advance, to probe any weak spots. Try to lead the witness gradually around to your point of view, but do not confuse expressing your point of view with putting questions to the witness. You want to keep asking questions which will gradually lead the witness to a conclusion which is your point. You will not get there if you tell the witness at the start what it is.

3.   During the inquiry, keep track of any points the witness may concede in cross examination by the LPA's advocate. If a point is conceded, note it down for further reference. There is no need to get the witness to concede it again to you, and you do not need to put questions on that same point or points. The inspector will have noted the witness's concession.

4.   If a development proposal is likely to have sufficiently far reaching environmental consequences to require the preparation of an assessment, it follows you are unlikely to

be the only person affected. Get someone else to make a note while you are asking questions if possible. It is extremely difficult to do both at once.

5.   Avoid making a political statement when questioning the witness, because it will only irritate the inspector who may well stop you asking questions if it appears you are wasting time at public expense with matters which he or she cannot take into consideration. The inspector has power to expel anyone who is disruptive.

People rightly feel strongly about environmental issues – the chances are the inspector has his or her own views like everyone else – but the purpose of the inquiry is to examine the relevant planning issues, not the state of your or anyone's passions on the subject. Stick to points about the weaknesses in the environmental statement whatever the temptation to do otherwise.

Environmental assessments now required in some enforcement appeals

In all enforcement notice appeals there is a deemed application for planning permission for the activity or development constituting the breach of planning control being enforced against. If the breach involves development which would require an environmental assessment under Schedule 1, or if it is a type specified by Schedule 2 for which the LPA would require an environmental assessment if a planning permission were sought, the developer must submit an environmental assessment in connection with the deemed application.

The badgers felt their views had been insufficiently represented at the motorway inquiry

12

Motorways

As anyone who regularly watches television or reads the newspapers knows, few types of development have aroused a greater public response in recent years than motorway proposals. Although objectors seem to receive the bulk of the media coverage, what often goes unreported is the fact that motorway proposals have many supporters. Motorway proposals are put forward by the Department of Transport in response to an identified need or to alleviate an identified problem. This is an important point which needs to be appreciated by anyone affected by a motorway proposal, who wishes to make representations for or against the scheme.

In the case of motorways, the planning cake analogy may be used, because although motorways are built with reference to different legislation, there are the same legal, government policy and public consultation.

Roles of the Secretary of State for Transport and the Secretary of State for the Environment

The Secretary of State for Ttransport 'proposes' new motorway development for stated reasons and will ultimately decide whether or not to proceed with the proposal in conjunction with the Secretary of State for the Environment. The decision to proceed, amend or even consider amending the proposed scheme will depend to some extent on what objections to the proposal have been sustained in the public consultation process as weighed against the need for the new road.

Many people who have been adversely affected by motorway proposals, or have watched with horror as new motorways cut a swathe across the countryside believe – not without justification – that it is next to impossible to affect a political decision to build roads.

That is not always the case, however, and certainly it is true to say that if those with views on new roads do not avail themselves of the public consultation process to make their representations heard, they will definitely not be in a position to affect the decision making process.

How the legal, government policy and public consultation elements apply

A road scheme begins with an 'order' under the 1980 Highways Act. This order must be confirmed by the Secretaries of State at the end of the public consultation period prescribed by the Act. The order when drawn up will take account of central government policies which are applicable (if for example the road will affect historic villages or areas of outstanding natural beauty).

The Highways Agency prepares the order and carries out all research which appears to be appropriate to investigate both the need for the scheme and the effects it will have. For example, an environmental assessment will be made.

The order for the scheme is prepared in draft form. This shows the route or the 'line' (this means the centre line) the road will follow. At the same time, it prepares such draft compulsory purchase orders under the 1981 Land Acquisition Act as may be necessary to build the road.

It is important to remember these draft orders are not in themselves law, although they are prepared within a legal framework. They are then 'published' for public consultation. This means they are advertised and displayed publicly, and any individual, group or statutory undertaker – such as English Heritage, English Nature, the National Rivers Authority, British Rail, etc. – has an opportunity to study the draft, see how they will be affected and make representations accordingly.

The Highways Act provides the Secretary of State with power to hold a public inquiry if there remain unresolved public objections to the scheme. There is further power under the Acquisition of Land Act to hold public inquiries into such draft compulsory purchase orders necessary to obtain the land required for the highway scheme.

Public consultation

A considerable amount of work will have gone into the preparation of the draft order. The starting point, or the identified need for the highway will be published as the reasons for the order. This may be that traffic needs to be routed out of a town centre or away from residential areas, for sound environmental reasons, or to provide a new or improved transport route between A and B.

An environmental impact assessment will have been prepared, together with traffic studies and a host of other background material. In many cases more than one potential route will have been considered in the preparation of the draft order. Those other potential routes will also have been made available and public response to them invited.

The exercise will obviously involve the balancing of a variety of interests, economic and environmental. People living in towns and residential areas on urban fringes may well have a strong case that the noise, pollution and traffic jams caused by through traffic in their areas ought to be moved to an out of town location, such as a bypass. Businesses wishing to transport goods from A to B need a quick and efficient commercial route for their lorries, and anyone whose job depends on the manufacture and transport of those goods will have a similar interest.

It is a forgone conclusion that the ultimate solution is unlikely to please everyone, and indeed may leave many people dissatisfied. To some extent the route chosen for a new motorway may mean choosing the lesser of two evils. The point of the public consultation exercise is to clarify to the fullest extent possible the factual basis for the objections to the route indicated on the draft order.

Inquiries into orders

When the draft order is 'published', it and all the accompanying documents and plans will be displayed in a location open to the public. Anyone who is potentially affected will wish to see the plans and the material which accompanies them. There will also be a statement of the Department's reasons for proposing the scheme.

It is the job of the Highways Agency to promote the scheme and to handle all the arrangements for public consultation at different stages.

Anyone who goes along to inspect the plans will find information available to explain the scheme and where objections should be sent and what the closing date is for receiving them.

If there are unresolved objections to the scheme the Secretary of State orders a public inquiry to be held. If there is to be an inquiry, this will be announced within four weeks of the expiry of the period for objections.

Purpose of the inquiry

Unlike planning or enforcement appeal inquiries which take into account the merits of a proposal, the development plan and all material considerations, the focus of a motorway inquiry is different. The purpose is to examine the objections in the light of the reasons given by the Highways Agency as to why the proposal is necessary. At the same time the inquiry can examine the evidence on matters relevant to compulsory purchase orders, such as whether more land is to be compulsorily purchased than is actually needed for the proposal.

Unlike planning inspectors who are appointed by the DoE, the inspector at a motorway inquiry is appointed by the Lord Chancellor. The inspector will hear all the evidence and report on it and his or her conclusions as to whether the order should be confirmed to the Secretary of State. The Secretaries of State for the Environment and Transport make the final decision jointly.

Rules governing inquiry procedure

These are the Highways (Inquiries Procedure) Rules 1994, and if one or more compulsory purchase orders are involved, the Compulsory Purchase by Ministers (Inquiries Procedure) Rules 1994.

Anyone contemplating an appearance to present a case at a motorway inquiry will probably find it helpful to obtain a copy of these rules. They are very much in line with the procedure for planning inquiries, but the pre-inquiry procedures have a more formal status and must be carefully observed.

Who may appear at a motorway inquiry?

The rules allow certain parties to appear as of right. These include statutory bodies and any individuals or groups of individuals directly affected by the proposal. This includes bodies such as residents' associations or local amenity societies.

In practice however, as with planning inquiries, the inspector is most unlikely to deny anyone who wishes to speak an opportunity to do so. However, if the inspector is confronted with 'rent-a-crowd' objectors who appear to be wasting the inquiry's time with obstructive tactics or making irrelevant or repetitious points, he or she may decline to hear them further or require them to leave the inquiry.

Pre-inquiry procedure

By reason of the size of a motorway proposal, the many interests of both private parties and statutory bodies affected, and the inevitable volume and complexity of the evidence involved, motorway inquiries can go on for many months, and in some cases years. Anyone who has ever attended a lengthy motorway inquiry may feel this says a great deal about the stamina of the inspectors appointed to conduct the inquiry, but it also attests to the fact that a vast amount of taxpayers' money stands to be spent in the process.

Inquiries must be conducted in a fair, open and impartial way, to allow everyone who wishes to be consulted an opportunity to be heard. At the same time, public inquiries take place at public expense and the inspector will apply the procedural rules in such a way as to ensure time is not wasted.

The rules are intended to streamline, to the fullest extent possible, what actually takes place at the inquiry, and to ensure that only matters pertaining to objections are explored (although part of this process may involve supporters putting their case and responding to objections). Any part of the scheme which is not contentious does not need to be explored in the inquiry.

Statements of case

Once it has been announced an inquiry will be held, anyone who has written to object to the draft order will receive an outline statement of case from the Highways Agency, usually within eight weeks, explaining why the particular route was chosen. Objectors and supporters must prepare and submit their own outline statements of case within a further time period specified by the agency.

Proofs of evidence and summaries

As in planning inquiries, the parties exchange proofs of evidence before the inquiry. Any proofs over 1500 words will need to be accompanied by a summary of no more than that length. The summary will be read out at the inquiry but the witness will be cross examined on the full proof. The inspector will have taken the full proof into account when writing the report.

Pre-inquiry meeting

The Highways Agency will give third party objectors and supporters three weeks' notice if it is decided to hold a pre-inquiry meeting. The purpose of a pre-inquiry meeting is to allow the inspector to deal with organizational matters, such as the order in which cases will be heard and a provisional timetable for witnesses to be called. Parties will be informed of the arrangements made for a library of the documents at the inquiry and where they may find photocopying facilities and whether there will be evening sittings.

Given that the inquiry is likely to be a long one, it is unlikely that most third parties will wish or be able to attend every day. The pre-inquiry meeting will indicate roughly when the objector can expect to be called, but this is subject to a degree of variation depending on the length of time taken by other parties in cross examination or unexpected matters which need to be dealt with by the inspector.

The programme officer

It is a good idea to make friends with the programme officer. The Highways Agency appoint a programme officer for long inquiries to keep things running smoothly and to act as a liaison between the inspector and objectors. Any matters of timing or administration should be taken up with him or her. Anyone who is unsure about procedure or any aspect of the inquiry will find the programme officer a valuable source of information and help.

No one should be shy about asking for help about procedure, documents or anything else. Motorway inquires may seem daunting but they are intended to provide those affected by the draft order with an opportunity to test the case put forward on its behalf. If it is possible to attend for a few sessions before giving evidence, the procedures at the inquiry will soon seem familiar.

The programme officer will keep track of the schedule for the inquiry and by the week's end will normally have prepared a timetable for the following week. Anyone who wants to know from the provisional timetable when they are likely to be able to cross examine an opposing witness or present evidence should check with the programme officer.

Procedure at the inquiry

Procedure at motorway inquiries is virtually the same as planning inquiry procedure. The main difference in substance is that the issues in a motorway inquiry are the objections. The main difference in practical terms is that a motorway inquiry is likely to be much larger, involve more parties, and more documents, many of which will be of a technical nature.

The inspector will open the inquiry and formally take appearances of all parties formally appearing. He or she will then ask if anyone else wishes to speak and will note the names of anyone who does so, in order that that person can be assured of an appropriate time slot. Anyone who wishes to know what has happened on previous days will be able to obtain a transcript of the proceedings if the inquiry is likely to be sitting for more than 15 days. This will enable anyone who is giving evidence or presenting a case to know what the Highways Agency's witness has already said in cross examination.

It is important to remember that the inquiry is not an adversarial contest. It is intended to clarify those matters of fact which are in dispute relevant to whether the draft order should be confirmed, because it is important that it be confirmed on a factually correct basis.

(i) The Highways Agency open their case at the inquiry

The Highways Agency will be represented by experienced planning counsel approved by the Attorney General. Counsel for the Agency will make an opening speech outlining the reasons the route was chosen and indicating briefly what problems have been identified which the new scheme is designed to eliminate. Counsel will also refer to any measures which may be proposed to minimize any harm caused by the proposal. Anyone planning to present a case will find it helpful to hear the opening statement, even if they are unlikely to attend every session of the inquiry.

Unless the inspector decides there is some advantage in hearing the proof of evidence in full, the Agency's witness will read the summary only. However, objectors – and the inspector – will have a copy of the full proof and the full proof is the subject of the cross examination.

In order to prepare a cross examination thoroughly it may be necessary to have referred in advance to certain of the other inquiry documents, such as the environmental statement, which will be available in the library being kept for the inquiry.

(ii) Supporters' case

Although the purpose of the inquiry is to examine the factual basis for objections, supporters may also make a formal appearance. They may be professionally represented or may choose to represent themselves, and may call expert witnesses. The point of their appearance is to respond to objections which have been raised.

Objectors should not ignore the case being put by supporters, as some element may prove relevant to a particular objection. For example, a supporter may concede an objection is valid on certain grounds, and vice versa.

Policy considerations

Anyone objecting to the Agency's case for the draft proposal should consider what government policy considerations apply in the circumstances. For example, if the objectors' case is that the draft proposal affects an area of outstanding natural beauty, a green belt or listed buildings, it will be important to refer to the relevant provisions of the appropriate government policy document. This will be either the relevant planning policy guidance or DoE circular. These will in all probability be available in the inquiry library.

It is important to remember that the inspector will base his or her recommendations to the Secretaries of State on the evidence at the inquiry. Any evidence, whether of the Highways Agency witnesses or of objectors, which does not stand up in cross examination will be noted in the inspector's report and the Secretary of State will be advised to discount it accordingly.

If a point has already been conceded there is no need for further examination on it. For further advice on cross examination technique, see the section on Cross examination in planning inquiries, page 72, and Questioning the developer's environmental witness, page 144 in Chapter 11.

Alternative routes

In many cases the Agency have considered more than one route and have rejected alternatives in favour of the one shown on the draft order. Objectors who feel one of these alternative routes would be preferable can cross examine the agency on the reasons it was not considered or if considered, why not adopted in preference to the draft route.

If a government policy supports a case for an alternative route it should be raised in cross examination.

It may also be possible to suggest a route no one has considered. If there is a case to be made that an alternative route would be more in keeping with government policy, this can be put to the Agency's witness.

Objectors' case

Objectors may represent themselves, appoint one of their number to act as spokesperson or engage a professional representative. They may call expert witnesses. Objectors do not make an opening speech.

Objectors will read their summaries of evidence unless the inspector decides the proof should be read in full. If several objectors wish to make the same points, it is sensible for one to be appointed as spokesperson for the group. The inspector will be very conscious of wasting time by repetitious evidence.

Cross examination of objectors

Objectors can expect to be thoroughly cross examined by barristers experienced in motorway inquiries who are acting for the Highways Agency. This can be a gruelling experience for someone who does not know what to expect, and for this reason it will be helpful to watch the Agency's cross examination of other witnesses. It is also important to have thought the case through and prepared the proof carefully, with an eye to spotting the weak points before they are winkled out in cross examinations. The best advice is to keep calm, no matter how forceful the cross examining counsel becomes. Knowing a case thoroughly is the best way of boosting confidence.

Closing speeches

If someone has appeared at the inquiry to speak briefly for or against the proposal, there is no need to worry about making a closing speech. The inspector will have the points.

However, for parties putting in a formal appearance, a good closing speech is very important because it pulls a case together, weighing the merits and evidence which supports that case against the case made by the opponents.

An effective closing speech will be prepared with regard for what evidence has stood up to cross examination and what points have been conceded in the course of the inquiry. How has this narrowed the issues in dispute? What effect has this had on the cases being presented?

Finally, the closing speech must emphasize the merits of the case on behalf of which it is made and point out the shortcomings of the case or cases put by opponents.

Objectors normally go first in closing speeches. The Highways Agency goes last, and effectively gets the last word.

Tips for preparing a closing speech

- Begin by making an outline of their case and your case. (Leave plenty of space between each point because you will need to fill it in later.) They say A, B and C, we say they are wrong because of X, Y, and Z.

- Look at the evidence. Get a red and green marker and underline points which have been sustained or arisen in cross examination which favour the case you are making in green, the oppositions points which still stand against you in red.

- Try to formulate the case you are making in a sentence or two when beginning your closing speech: 'Our case at this inquiry is that in proposing this particular route through an area of outstanding natural beauty, the promoters (the Highways Agency) have failed to apply Government policy that new motorways should have as little impact as possible on AONBs. The evidence supports our contention that another route to meet the same objectives of the proposed scheme would be preferable. In the circumstances it would be appropriate for the inspector to recommend to the Secretary of State that a more appropriate alternative ought to be considered.' This gives the inspector a coherent framework for your speech and the points you want to make.

- Return to your outline. Look at how government policy applies. What does the evidence say about the way it been applied? Slot this into your outline where appropriate. You may have to acknowledge that on the evidence the other side has taken some part of the policy into account but not in its entirety.

- As a matter of tactics it is preferable to acknowledge any points where your case is weak and discount them before the other side raises them.

- If it is possible to anticipate, and discredit in advance what the other side is likely to say, this is also a good tactic.

- Emphasize the merits of your case and the lack of merit in your opponents' case.

- If there is a balance which must be achieved as between objectives, say why the balance ought to be exercised in your favour.

- Go over the outline several times. Write out the closing

speech based on the outline. Make sure you have not reiterated all the evidence – you need only highlight the essential points to your case. Check for repetition.

- If you know that another party will be making some of the same points in putting a similar case, there is no need to repeat them in yours. You can tell the inspector you concur with what has already been said in closing on a particular point.
- Remember that few closing speeches will fail to benefit from editing – probably several times. The more coherent, concise and well organized the closing speech, the more helpful it will be to the inspector.
- What you do not want to do is leave the inspector wondering what you were getting at.

The site visit

After all closing speeches have been heard, the inspector will announce what arrangements have been made for a formal site visit. On this he or she is accompanied by a representative from the Highways Agency and one or more objectors. Anyone else who wishes to be present may probably be so. However, it is essential that no party attempt to make any further submissions, introduce further evidence or 'get the inspector's ear'. The inspector is strictly concerned only with viewing the site and will scrupulously avoid even the appearance of behaving in a less than even-handed manner.

Planning permission for a Bell ringing school proves upsetting for local residents.

13

Compensation

Some planning decisions can result in an owner, occupier, or anyone else with an interest in the land receiving compensation, either because they have been forced to part with the land altogether or because a planning decision has affected the value of the land, and restricted the ways in which the land can be used.

The interests in the land which qualify for compensation if they are affected and the circumstances which must apply before compensation is payable are somewhat complex in each case.

Broadly speaking, in the planning system, compensation arises in the following ways:

Compulsory purchase notices

Compulsory purchase notices enable acquisition of land required for public development or other public purposes by the LPA or the Secretary of State.

There are circumstances in which the LPA or the government may forcibly buy land.

Compulsory acquisition of land by the LPA

If land is required for some specific form of public development, or for some other public purpose, LPAs may acquire the land by agreement with the owner or seek to compel the acquisition by serving a compulsory purchase notice (CPO) on the owner, occupier or lessee. In most cases this will not come as a surprise as the party or parties affected will usually have been aware of the possibility. The CPO must then be confirmed by the Secretary of State before it is effective.

The CPO notice must specify the land to which the notice relates and the reason the LPA are seeking to acquire the land. The CPO must also specify the reasons or purposes for which the land is being acquired, inform the person on whom the notice is served of the right to object to the notice within a specified time and where the objections must be sent.

There are four circumstances in which the LPA may seek to acquire property in this way:

- to obtain land for the purpose of carrying out development, re-development or improvement (for example, town centre re-development). If land is acquired for this purpose, the LPA must offer to relocate on the land affected anyone formerly living or carrying on a business on that site;
- for some other purpose in the interest of proper planning where land is not required for development, redevelopment or improvement (for example, land for access or amenity or to prevent inappropriate development taking place);
- land required for facilitative works on land acquired through compulsory purchase to carry out development, re-development or improvement. In these cases the LPA must offer relocation on the land to existing persons living or carrying on businesses on the land;
- land required for the purpose of exchange for any common land, open space or allotment land being compulsorily purchased.

When the LPA serves, and the Secretary of State considers, whether or not to confirm a CPO, both must take into account the provisions of the development plan and all other material considerations. The considerations are similar to those which arise in respect of an application for planning permission (save that government policy also requires that individual applications for planning permission be considered on their merits).

The LPA must not use the CPO process to acquire land for development, re-development, improvement or any of the other purposes if what the LPA proposes to do with the land is development contrary to the development plan or would be barred by other material considerations.

Compulsory acquisition of land by the Secretary of State for planning purposes

The Secretary of State has like powers to those of the LPA to acquire land by CPO for the same purposes. One example of land acquired for such purposes is land necessary for a motorway development scheme (see Chapter 12).

If the person(s) on whom the CPO is served have objections (and they are not objections the Secretary of State regards as solely related to the amount of compensation to be paid) to the CPO, the Secretary of State may order a public inquiry.

Right to appeal against a CPO

Anyone who is served with a CPO, either by the LPA or the Secretary of State will be informed in due course of the procedure for appealing against it before it is confirmed.

If the CPO is served by the LPA, the appeal will be very similar to a planning appeal. (see Planning appeals, page 32). The appellant will be concerned why the reason given for

Purchase Notice
Palmerston Council)
Town and Country Planning Act 1971
Purchase Notice (section 180)

To the Chief Executive and Clerk of ....
With reference to land
at.. subject
of a planning decision, reference ....by...........................
dated...................... (subject to an appeal to the Secretary of State, reference.................. , the decision on which was dated...............), refusing
planning permission or granting planning permission subject to conditions.

I/We serve notice, under section 180 of the Town and Country Planning Act
1971, on the Council of............ : and I/we claim that:
(a)   the land has become incapable of reasonably beneficial use in its
        existing state, and
(b)   it cannot be rendered capable of reasonably beneficial use by the
        carrying out of the development for which Permission was granted in
        accordance with the conditions imposed, and
(c)   it cannot be rendered capable of reasonably beneficial use by the
        carrying out of any other development for which permission has been
        granted or is deemed to be granted, or for which the local planning
        authority or the Secretary of State have undertaken to grant
        permission; and

I/We hereby require the Council to purchase my/our interest in the said
land,namely ....
....
....
Full name(s) and address(es) of owner(s)

....

Signature(s)..
Date..
Agents ....
Telephone No.......................................
Reference ....

Figure 7 Compulsory Purchase Notice (Based on DoE Circular
13/83 and Welsh Office Circular 22/83. Crown copyright)

serving the notice is to facilitate development contra-indicated by the development plan and all other material considerations (for example, the effect on listed buildings or their settings).

If the CPO is served by the Secretary of State, the recipient will have a more difficult job, because the CPO is likely to have been served in connection with a major public development project, such as a motorway or airport (see Chapter 12). Any objections to a CPO served for this purpose will be explored in the course of the public inquiry ordered to inquire into the unresolved objections to the development itself.

Compensation paid under a CPO

The compensation which is payable for land acquired by CPO is the 'market value' of the land. The Lands Tribunal have jurisdiction to determine any disputes arising as to the amount of compensation.

Purchase notices

This is like a form of CPO in reverse, by which the owner or occupier of land may require the LPA to purchase land because planning permission has either been refused, or has been granted subject to onerous conditions, or if planning permission has been revoked or modified after being granted.

This procedure is not available to every owner of land dissatisfied by a planning decision. Broadly speaking, such claims depend upon:

- the land being 'incapable of beneficial use' as it is,

and

- if conditional permission was granted, the conditions are such that even if the permission were implemented with the conditions, the land would still be incapable of beneficial use.

Anyone who believes they may be entitled to serve a purchase notice on the LPA should contact the LPA for a 'Purchase notice' form. Any purchase notice must be served on the LPA within 12 months of the refusal of permission or the grant of conditional permission.

The LPA may either accept or reject the purchase notice. If it rejects it, the notice must be referred to the Secretary of State who may confirm or reject the notice. Before he or she does either, the landowner and the LPA will be notified of his intention, and if either wish, a public inquiry will be held before the Secretary of State decides.

Planning blight

In contrast to circumstances in which an owner of land may be able to require the LPA to purchase his land as the result of a refusal of permission or the grant of an unviable conditional permission, the owner or occupier of land affected by a proposed scheme for some form of public development – although the land is not actually required for that development – may be able to require the LPA to acquire his or her land if the market value of the land has been markedly affected or 'blighted' by the proposal. This might apply to people living near a proposed motorway, for example.

However, given that there is potentially a very large group of people who might come forward claiming their land would be blighted by any public works project, the statutory provisions are complex and restrictive as to who qualifies, and in what circumstances, for compensation for 'blight'.

The procedure for blight notices is similar to the purchase notice procedure in that a blight notice is served on the LPA or appropriate government body responsible for the blighting development. If the LPA or government body object to the blight notice, they serve a counter notice specifying what their objections are.

In this case the claimant has no right to a public inquiry. Instead, counter notices may be referred to the Lands Tribunal within two months. The Lands Tribunal will then determine whether or not compensation is payable, depending on the claim and the reasons for rejecting it. A failure to refer the counter notice means that it becomes effective and the authority is not obliged to compensate the claimant.

14

Where To Go for Further Information and Advice

While this book is intended to provide sufficient guidance to enable people to cope with a range of planning matters and problems, there will still be cases where, for various reasons, those dealing with a planning matter will wish to or should seek further advice and assistance. Undeniably, some planning matters have such a complex but highly relevant planning history that they throw up a veritable Gordian knot of complications which may need to be unravelled before anyone can deal with the present problem. It may also happen that the planning matter in question has been the subject of case law which needs to be taken into account because it is relevant to the problem. Finally, dealing with planning matters is undeniably time consuming, and it may be more economic to seek professional advice, or hand the matter over to professionals entirely.

This section tells you where to go for further help, what to look for when seeking it, and what you can do to ensure the assistance you obtain meets your needs as fully and economically as possible.

Professional Advisors

There are three main types of professionals who can be engaged to deal with a planning matter: solicitors, barristers and planning consultants. The first two categories, obviously, are legally trained, while planning consultants are not. However, they will necessarily be conversant with planning legislation. Remember that unlike matters involving court proceedings, there is nothing to prevent anyone appearing on behalf of any party at a public inquiry, or indeed giving advice on planning matters. If you are contemplating seeking advice or assistance from anyone holding himself or herself out as offering some degree of planning expertise, it is probably a good idea to check out his or her qualifications and experience first.

Solicitors

Whether or not you propose using a barrister as well, anyone who feels legal advice is required on a planning matter will normally begin by going to a solicitor. In most cases, barristers can only be instructed by solicitors and not by clients directly (save in some limited circumstances where this rule has been relaxed in recent years).

As with doctors – or indeed any professional – the best advice is 'horses for courses'. No one seeks advice on hip replacements from an obstetrician, or expects a GP to perform open heart surgery, yet while people know all doctors are not qualified to be all things to all people, it is surprising how often they fail to appreciate that the same applies to lawyers.

The same lawyer who did such a brilliant job on your business lease/divorce settlement/or getting you out of jail cannot reasonably be expected to be an instant authority on all aspects of planning law as well. Large urban law firms often have a specialist, or in some cases, a whole department, to handle planning and associated matters. Smaller firms or individual practitioners may or may not know anything about planning. It is always advisable to shop around for expert assistance, and it does not cost anything to ring up a solicitor or firm of solicitors and ask if planning is one of their specialities.

Solicitors do not come cheap – most charge by the hour – and it makes little sense to hire someone who will have to spend time swotting up on an unknown area of law at your expense.

It is advisable to ask if the solicitor or firm have an up to date copy of *The Planning Encyclopaedia* (published by Sweet & Maxwell and updated at regular intervals as appropriate) in the office or can get hold of one if necessary. It is sometimes the case that while a solicitor does deal with planning matters on a very occasional basis – in which case he or she probably passes them on to a planning consultant or barrister – there is no *Planning Encyclopaedia* available if something crops up which needs to be checked (*The Planning Encyclopedia*, published by Sweet and Maxwell, is *the* practitioners' Bible – be wary if your consultant tells you it makes no difference whether or not it is available).

Having found a solicitor, ask whether your problem is one the solicitor can deal with and how much it is likely to cost. It can often be cheaper and more cost effective in the long run for the solicitor and you to hire a barrister or planning consultant. For example, if the solicitor is a member of a small firm or a single practitioner, he or she may find it is difficult to be tied up for one or more full days in a planning inquiry while other work is pending.

On the other hand, in some areas of the country, particularly where there is ongoing pressure for a particular type of development, some local solicitors have developed an extensive knowledge of local planning history and issues and a planning expertise particularly suited to the area.

Once you have shopped around and found a solicitor knowledgeable about planning law, you will save everyone's time and your money if you prepare very carefully before an initial appointment to explain your problem. Set out in a short written document what it is you want to build/object to or otherwise what the problem is as you see it. Check with the LPA to see what they say about the matter (that is free). Make copies of any relevant documents, such as former planning permissions, a planning application, notice of refusal, enforcement notice, etc., and arrange them in chronological order. Note whether the area concerned has any special features such as listed buildings or is in a green belt or conservation area. Ask the LPA about policies in the development plan or go through it yourself.

Think about the matter on which you are seeking advice. How would you sum it up in one complete sentence? This may sound very basic, particularly if you have read the rest of this book, but all professionals – solicitors, barristers and planning consultants alike – can attest to cases where a great deal of time is spent unnecessarily at the outset trying to pin down precisely what the problem is they are being asked to deal with. They then have to follow this up researching precisely the type of information the client can easily come prepared with – information which the client had at his or her fingertips all along but either did not bother, or felt too shy, to disclose.

There is absolutely no point in engaging a professional to write a lengthy report at your expense to tell you what you already know. Therefore, to the extent possible, narrow down the issue or questions on which you are seeking advice.

Your solicitor or planning consultant may feel it would be advisable to seek a barrister's advice on your planning problem before deciding what to do next. This is known as 'taking Counsel's opinion' and will normally be advised in circumstances where the legal position about some element of your planning matter is unclear – for example if your solicitor thinks the LPA may be wrong about the legal implications of some past development or permission granted on your property.

Alternatively, you may wish a barrister or solicitor to take over your the matter entirely. If so, ask about fees in advance.

Barristers

You cannot approach a barrister directly. Until recently a barrister could only be instructed by a solicitor, but recent changes in the professional rules have now made it possible for barristers to be instructed directly by planning consultants as well.

The planning consultant or solicitor you have consulted initially may well have a particular barrister or set of chambers in mind, who are known to be planning specialists. Obviously there is no point seeking planning advice from a specialist in crime or matrimonial law, but these days most chambers advertise the areas of law in which their members specialize. The consultant or solicitor instructing counsel will have to go through the barrister's clerk, who will negotiate a fee for the opinion or for taking over conduct of the planning matter (but remember that the solicitor/planning consultant does not bow out at this stage – you will still be paying for their involvement).

If you have prepared thoroughly for your initial consultation with the solicitor or planning consultant, this will make it easier for whoever is instructing counsel to pass on clear and concise instructions about your planning matter and all the relevant material.

Planning consultants

Planning consultants can have a range of experience and expertise. For example, some leading consultants have experience in local authority planning departments which can be particularly useful in some cases. Consultants may also have a particular speciality – shopping centres, motorways or green belts, or areas of archaeological importance, for example, perhaps because a firm has done a particular type of work of this kind in different parts of the country. Ask in advance about qualifications, particular expertise and fees, and prepare as much of the relevant information as possible.

The Royal Town Planning Institute can be contacted for names of planning consultants in your area. Their address is:

Royal Town Planning Institute
26 Portland Place
London
W1N 4BE

Other sources of planning assistance

There are other sources of help with planning matters for those unable to instruct professional help themselves.

Regional Planning Aid Service

There is a charitable organization, funded in part by the Royal Town Planning Institute, which can in some cases provide advice and assistance with planning matters for no charge or for a small contribution. They can provide a wide range of assistance to both groups and individuals, from telephone advice to witnesses at public inquiries. However, they may not be able to help in every case and, where appropriate, may charge a fee.

For further information, including information about whether the service is available in your area of the country, contact:

Planning Aid for London
Calvert House
5 Calvert Avenue
London
E2 7JP
Tel: 0171 613 4435

Law centres

Whether local law centres can assist with planning matters depends very much on the resources available and the demand for this advice in the locality. However, there is nothing wrong with contacting your local law centre to inquire. Many law centres have a pool of volunteers – normally solicitors or barristers who may donate their services free of charge for an hour or two each week. If there is likely to be a major demand for planning advice – for example, because a motorway or other large development is proposed – it may be that the law centre can arrange an advice session with someone who specializes in planning law.

Alternatively, a law centre may have, or have access to, a copy of *The Planning Encyclopaedia* or be able to tell you where to find one. It does not cost anything to ask, and even if there is no lawyer to give advice, you may be able to look up the planning topic you wish to deal with and find the information you want yourself.

Citizens Advice Bureaux

Whether or not a CAB can help with a planning matter will probably depend on how much demand there is for such advice in the area. It costs nothing to ask, and the CAB may have a copy of *The Planning Encyclopaedia* or know where you can find one.

Seeking further help: checklists

Before seeking professional advice:

- Obtain the planning history of the site from the LPA.
- Be prepared with all relevant facts about the planning matter.
- Ascertain whether there are any special features which affect the planning status of the site.
- Make copies of all relevant documents, plans, previous permissions or planning decisions, including any decisions by planning inspectors.
- Find out what development plan policies apply, and make a copy.
- Seek the views of the LPA as relevant.

When seeking professional advice:

- Be prepared to explain briefly what the matter is on which advice is being sought.
- Ask whether this is the sort of matter the firm or individual deal with.

— Enquire about fees – are they charged by the hour? is there a scale of fees? etc.

— Consider whether an initial consultation would help in determining how much more assistance would be required.

— Check whether the professional whose advice you are seeking has access to an up to date copy of *The Planning Encyclopaedia*.